KU-608-634

The Bloke's Guide
to Babies

The Bloke's Guide to Babies

Jon Smith

HAY HOUSE

Australia • Canada • Hong Kong • India
South Africa • United Kingdom • United States

First published and distributed in the United Kingdom by:
Hay House UK Ltd, 292B Kensal Rd, London W10 5BE.
Tel.: (44) 20 8962 1230; Fax: (44) 20 8962 1239. www.hayhouse.co.uk

Published and distributed in the United States of America by:
Hay House, Inc., PO Box 5100, Carlsbad, CA 92018-5100.
Tel.: (1) 760 431 7695 or (800) 654 5126;
Fax (1) 760 431 6948 or (800) 650 5115. www.hayhouse.com

Published and distributed in Australia by:
Hay House Australia Ltd, 18/36 Ralph St, Alexandria NSW 2015.
Tel.: (61) 2 9669 4299; Fax: (61) 2 9669 4144. www.hayhouse.com.au

Published and distributed in the Republic of South Africa by:
Hay House SA (Pty), Ltd, PO Box 990, Witkoppen 2068.
Tel./Fax: (27) 11 467 8904. www.hayhouse.co.za

Published and distributed in India by:
Hay House Publishers India, Muskaan Complex, Plot No.3, B-2, Vasant Kunj, New
Delhi – 110 070. Tel.: (91) 11 41761620; Fax: (91) 11 41761630. www.hayhouse.co.in

Distributed in Canada by:
Raincoast, 9050 Shaughnessy St, Vancouver, BC V6P 6E5.
Tel.: (1) 604 323 7100; Fax: (1) 604 323 2600

© Jon Smith, 2008

Reprinted 2010

The moral rights of the author have been asserted.

All rights reserved. No part of this book may be reproduced by any mechanical,
photographic or electronic process, or in the form of a phonographic recording;
nor may it be stored in a retrieval system, transmitted or otherwise be copied for
public or private use, other than for 'fair use' as brief quotations embodied in
articles and reviews, without prior written permission of the publisher.

The author of this book does not dispense medical advice or prescribe the use of
any technique as a form of treatment for physical or medical problems without the
advice of a physician, either directly or indirectly. The intent of the author is only
to offer information of a general nature to help you in your quest for emotional
and spiritual wellbeing. In the event you use any of the information in this book
for yourself, which is your constitutional right, the author and the publisher
assume no responsibility for your actions.

A catalogue record for this book is available from the British Library.

ISBN 978-1-4019-1609-1

Layout and Illustrations by Matt Windsor

Printed and bound in the UK by
TJ International Ltd, Padstow, Cornwall

Mixed Sources
Product group from well-managed
forests and other controlled sources
www.fsc.org Cert no. SGS-COC-2482
© 1996 Forest Stewardship Council

For Luka Zazzi and Mackenzie Harriman

Contents

About The Author

Jon Smith lives with his wife, Lisa, and their two children, Alia and Ronin. Jon writes books, screenplays and musical theatre.

Contact The Author

By Post
c/o Hay House
292b Kensal Road
London
W10 5BE
United Kingdom

By Email
jon@blokesguide.com

On The Web
www.blokesguide.com
www.justdads.co.uk

Acknowledgements

Extra-special thanks to: Malcolm, Chris Smith, Mark Mitchell, Andrew Zazzi. Mark Bevan, Owen Wainwright, Paul Critchley, Rhys Wilcox, Chris Hitchcock, Stephen Giles, Richard Burton.

Message to the Ladies

Your husband, boyfriend, partner, brother, uncle, friend – or whomever else you had in mind when you picked up this book – has just lived through the most exhilarating and scary experience of his life: a pregnancy and a birth. He took the bull by the horns and, we presume, he was there for his partner. All in all, the boy done good. But now the baby is back at home, and instead of relaxing, cracking open a nice bottle of red and congratulating himself on a job well done, he's worried again. Worried about what he needs to do next. Worried about when the crying is going to stop and worried about why he feels so ineffectual.

I'm guessing that your man gave a bravura performance during both the pregnancy and the birth and that it's obvious that he's determined to play an active part in the rearing of his child. After all, fatherhood, it is well documented, is a fantastic journey. But there are numerous things he needs to have answered, explained or illustrated before the man who will receive this book can feel in control enough to enjoy the experience.

If he's acting a bit like a spare part at the moment it's not that he's being deliberately obtuse about the baby, or that he is pretending to be completely incompetent or frightened – at least not consciously. He really is frightened... petrified, in fact. But that is the male reaction to anything we don't understand. Men need manuals: A + B = C. The hand is connected to the arm, which is connected to the shoulder, which is connected to the body – straightforward, to the point, and honest. Hence *The Bloke's Guide To Babies* – no flowery prose or idealistic diatribe, no Simon dressed as Simone. We want it raw and unabridged; tell us how it is. What's the worst can happen? What's the best that can happen? If the engine is smoking,

x

what should we look at first – the radiator or the alternator?

Yes, he might occasionally look at one of the numerous books written about parenting for women, (one of the five or so that you have already bought?) to read up on the deep science and follow the doctor's advice about what to do in such-and-such a situation – but they won't answer his questions. He wants the truth from a male perspective, in bite-size pieces that are as easy to digest as a tube of Pringles. (I didn't know paprika could taste so good.) This book tackles what *is* going on inside his head, not what *should* be going on. It is the product of over 80 interviews with blokes who have been there, done that and lived to tell the tale – and a few of them are full-time dads. So let us take the new father by his hand (metaphorically, of course!) and help him on his way.

He might even say thank you, and better yet, spend as much time with his child as you do.

Message to the Blokes

The Bloke's Guide to Babies is the culmination of numerous interviews with dads I conducted over a 12-month period. Although everyone's personal experiences will be unique, this book should come close to answering a lot of the questions that will arise over the course of your journey as a new father. All of the dads interviewed are experts. Maybe they don't have lots of letters after their names, but they've survived the first couple of years and were both willing and keen to try to help all of us dads out there who have recently had a little addition to the household.

After *The Bloke's Guide to Pregnancy* was published, I received a number of emails requesting more advice about what to do beyond birth. Basically, I didn't have a clue; I was only just experiencing it myself for the first time. Now, with a second child of my own to feed, house, school and to learn from, writing a follow-up book made a lot of sense; if nothing else I needed to find out some things for myself.

During Alia's and Ronin's formative months and years, as I was still coming to terms with being a dad, I would have found a book aimed at me very useful. But there wasn't much available when they were both little 9lb bundles of joy. So I hope that for many men about to embark on the trip that is fatherhood, this book will provide a bit of support.

If there is one piece of overriding advice that came through from my interviews it is simply this: go with your instinct, it will usually be right. But if you are looking for detail and expansion on certain points that have made us all question what on earth we are doing, then *The Bloke's Guide to Babies* is definitely your boy. Or girl... Ultimately you'll devise your own ways to entertain your baby and to deal with problems over the coming months and years, so don't be afraid to try new things. And above all enjoy every last minute, because it really does just fly past.

Chapter One

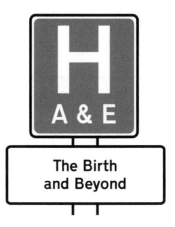

H
A & E

The Birth
and Beyond

So, How Was It for You?

So it's happened. After what seemed like an interminable
nine months, the baby is finally out, it's arrived, you made
it through unscathed (relatively) and unscarred... You're a
dad!

It terms of experiences, witnessing the birth of
your child is up there with the best of them. Words cannot
begin to explain what a profound physical and emotional
rollercoaster it is. Shocking, scary and beautiful, all at
once. A total-body experience – the sights, the sounds, the
smells, the sweat, the tears, the mucus, the blood, the
poo... granted we weren't the ones who *actually* gave birth,
but that doesn't mean we're any less traumatised.
Zazz explains:

How did I feel? Exhaustion and elation at the same time. Didn't really have a clue what I was doing but managed to keep the child alive. Nothing can really prepare you for the first days after the arrival, I especially remember changing a filthy, poo-filled nappy at 3am in February when the word 'dependent' took on a completely new meaning.

Chris, my brother and one of the many dads interviewed, thought he was prepared – he'd spent the past few months clocking up a number of vaginal births being shown on Sky's Baby Channel. But it's just not the same. Being in the room, feeling useless, anxious and a little nauseous, with your partner in so much pain – it's all so quick, so graphic... so real.

But you've done it. You survived. You're a dad! Hurrah! But what next?

Your Baby's First Few Hours

Sadly, the chances are that Mum and Baby are going to be stuck in hospital for at least a night or two, possibly more if there were any complications. Now, I've got every respect for health-care professionals, the same way I've got every respect for bank staff – they're paid to look after my assets, on my behalf, and they bring a wealth of experience to an operation which otherwise, left in my incompetent hands, would end in disaster. That said, with my baby born and my partner now stuck in 'stasis' in this foreign environment that is a hospital, I couldn't help feeling that I wanted the professional's involvement to stop. Right then. I wanted my partner and child back at home, with me. Don't get me wrong, if it could have been arranged I would have preferred a team of six or seven doctors to come back home with us, to check we were doing everything right. But I also wanted the environment to be comfortable and familiar and to drastically reduce the chances of one or both of my loved ones contracting MRSA or Legionnaire's, or having a kidney removed accidentally whilst under 'supervised care'.

Funnily enough, I was refused the six-strong retinue of doctors, so had to make do with a leaflet on *Contraception after Pregnancy and Birth*. A fair swap, methinks. My baby's been born, my wife's wearing a nightie with a split down the back, when can I bring them home?

Even more bizarrely, although Lisa was dead keen to come home, she actually admitted to enjoying 'hospital food', a phrase I had always thought was somewhat oxymoronic – but apparently the custard is 'to die for'. Stick around for a week of it and that's probably exactly what would happen...

Anyway, assuming you had a hospital birth, eventually (again assuming you're not forgotten about), you'll soon be discharged into the wild, wild world with your partner and baby. Fantastic. But why can't they let you go right now...?

Testing, Testing, 1-2-3

As if the trauma of birth wasn't enough stress in the last 24 hours, your baby needs to be tested before being unleashed to the world. These tests may happen over the course of the morning, in no particular order, by a number of different people, but they will be done. Here's a little bit about the most important ones:

The First Medical
The startle reflex

Sometimes referred to as the Moro Reflex, this is proof of evolution if ever you needed it. New babies startle easily – sudden movement, a loud noise, a sudden bright light or the feeling of falling should result in your baby being startled (funnily enough) and to spread out his arms. This natural reflex, which is evident for about the first six months, harps back to the days when Mum would have been covered in fur and referred to as a primate – she needed her own arms to move about, collect food and scratch. Baby would grip tightly to said fur and be carted around the place like Lady Muck.

So the science makes sense, although when you're witnessing it as one of Baby's first interactions with other humans, it's pretty scary.

Contorting hips

Just as he's recovered from the sheer terror of thinking he was falling, along comes the next test. Basically what the doctor's looking for here is whether the hip 'clicks' when the legs, or more accurately the hip joint, is manipulated. Lots of babies have clicky hips and in fact clicky knees and elbows. More often than not, it means nothing (most of my joints have always clicked – and that fad in the eighties we had of clicking our fingers together didn't do me many favours either), but if there's clicking it will be noted down and be looked at again at a clinic appointment in a few months' time.

Heartbeat

Having our heartbeat checked is something we've all experienced at least once and have seen on the telly so often that we can appreciate it's pretty much standard practice. The problem is that other than a cursory breath on the metal, courtesy of the kindly doctor, there is no warning to Baby that something very hard, metallic and *freezing cold* is going to be pushed onto his chest – the stethoscope may well be a great way to read a heartbeat, but it staggers me that the very action of using one hasn't caused more cardiac arrests.

The red reflex

There's nothing more to this than the shining of a bright light in Baby's eyes – OK, unpleasant, especially if they've woken her up just to do this test, but essential nonetheless – the doctor is checking the retina for a red reflex. If she has it, then she hasn't got cataracts. Simple as that.

So she's passed all her first tests with flying colours and then suddenly you are ushered out into the big wide world...

Home, James

'Best of luck; I'll just show you all to the door.'
'Yes, but what do we do when...'
'Bye!'

What? That's it? No manual? No escort home to check you're doing everything right? No forms to sign and no fee to be paid? What a strange, strange feeling. The long walk out of the hospital door, into the big bad world with a newborn baby, is about as terrifying as the birth itself. Why is everything so noisy? Who are these people smoking at the entrance? Get away from my pure, innocent, healthy child, you sick, slipper-wearing freak. Don't you dare reach out to touch my child with your unwashed, filth-ridden hands of death. Show some bloody respect!

There ensues a small altercation with the baby seat and some confusion over just *how* it fits into the car, now it's occupied. As the sweat beads begin to form on your brow, finally there's a resounding click of success. Fumbling in your pockets for change, thankfully for the last time in a while, you are free of the hospital car park and away. Cruising along at a deft ten miles per hour, the roads have never looked or felt so dangerous. A quick glance in the rear-view mirror reveals a tiny little body fast asleep and rocking violently to every bump in the far-from-satisfactory road on which you are driving. You might only have a 20-minute drive to get home but it feels like hours, and the sense of relief at safely arriving outside the house is almost orgasmic. Your body is screaming for a stiff Scotch, to steady the nerves, but the brain is telling you not to touch a drop. This is not funny in the slightest.

Slowly but surely you guide your war-worn partner gently into the house, supporting her every step of the way. The birth you have so recently witnessed is still very much in your mind's eye; only a matter of hours ago a new life entered the world and you witnessed it all. If it wasn't for the baby carrier and your bad knee, you'd be offering to carry her straight up to bed and insisting she rest for a couple of months. Then, unexpectedly, the pain kicks in. Why is it that the little bundle of joy lying so quietly in the baby seat suddenly weighs as much as a bag of cement? If you don't get in the house pretty sharpish, the weight is likely to rip the arm out of your socket. Eight pounds two ounces, my arse.

And There It Is

Baby is finally here. There is nothing more beautiful, pure and natural in the world. Fast asleep and, I'm afraid, your Lord (or Lady) forever more, whether you like it or not. In a strange way we all mess up. We read the books, even glance over a few of the pregnancy magazines that have taken up residence in your house over the last nine months – we go to the antenatal groups (and even pretend to enjoy them) and feel pretty confident about the whole pregnancy and birth thing. But therein lies the problem – what now? We were so hell-bent on understanding the process of birth, we forgot to investigate any further! What happens next? Suddenly a real baby is presented to you – your child – and it can bring back all those fears you had when you first learned that your partner was expecting a baby. Will I cope? Can we afford a child? Is my house big enough? Will I drop him?! Can I be an effective father? Worry not, dad, you'll be all right.

After the whirlwind of the birth, getting home with the newborn is probably the first time the three of you have sat together as a family without an audience. She sleeps as the two of you ponder the true impact of life with a newborn. Don't worry; the neighbours will give you precisely 15 minutes before the doorbell starts ringing, announcing the first of many, many well-wishers. Life will never, ever be the same again.

Chapter Two

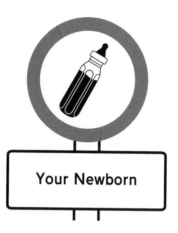

Your Newborn

Sleep Machine

Never have you met someone who can sleep as much as this. It's unbelievable. There you are, ready to play an all-night game of Dungeons & Dragons, followed by Buckaroo and a quick round of Twister if there's still time, and the main focus of your enthusiasm is having a kip. Again. In a way it's a good thing that newborns do sleep an awful lot, because the stress levels you can experience during the times they are awake can be tremendous. At times, you can almost feel the years dropping off your life expectancy. Nevertheless, you won't be the first dad to 'accidentally' bang around the house in an attempt to wake the child — you've been waiting nine months for this and you're still able to count on your fingers the number of cuddles you've had. It's hard, but leave them be. Your baby has just experienced the trauma of birth – head-first, probably – not to mention possibly being on a comedown from medical grade opiates. As if being squeezed through the birth canal wasn't enough, they've just had to come to grips with the art of breathing, processing their own waste, non-regulated ambient temperatures and a gaggle of grinning faces up close and personal, whose owners insist on making strange noises and then prodding, poking, touching and generally fussing. Sleep, it now becomes apparent, is probably a necessity and a welcome refuge.

Cry Baby

However, when they are awake they will cry. Unable to master their vocal cords, babies have only one way to communicate their every wish – by crying. A newborn baby's cry is pathetic. There's no two ways about it. It's a sound that you only need to hear once and it is instantly recognisable as your own infant's call. A call to action it is. The only problem is, *what* action?

'What's that, sweetheart? Did you just ask if it would be all right to have a bottle of warm breast milk, followed by a cuddle and a gentle rock, topped off with a light snooze, before a brisk walk in the park?'

Wrong. It was more like, *'Waaaaaaaaaaaagh.'* Breath. *'Waaaaaaaaaaaaaaaagh.'* Breath. Repeat.

Your baby will cry. And cry... and cry. Usually whenever you and your partner are trying to catch a bit of shut-eye yourselves. Crying is the only means of communication currently open to your child. Don't worry, it only lasts for about a year, by which stage your baby will be able to call the emergency services, by telephone, all by herself, whilst pressing play on *that* video you thought was successfully hidden under the sofa. Unable to do anything for themselves, babies rely on someone else (namely you and the missus) to provide them with the food, warmth and comfort that they need. Crying is a baby's way of communicating one or all of those needs. And within a few weeks you will begin to notice alterations in the tone and pitch of the cry that will usually (but not always) give you a clue as to what they are actually requesting.

Crying generally indicates one, or sometimes a combination, of the following:

Hunger
Easy to deal with. If breast-fed, pass the baby across to your partner and return to previous task. If bottle-fed, retrieve 'here's one I prepared earlier' from the fridge; heat, test and apply to Baby's mouth. Although hunger may not have been the root cause of the crying, for the duration of the feed peace will be returned to your home. This will be followed quickly by:

Nappy
Just as you would not enjoy festering in your own excrement, babies aren't too hot on the feeling either. As babies become toddlers there is no escaping the smell of poo and you react accordingly. However, very young baby poo does not always smell strongly enough to escape the nappy and therefore it is wise to have a quick peek if your baby is still crying. So now the nappy is all changed, but still she continues:

Ambience
Funnily enough, the very act of changing the nappy may have replaced one concern with another. After only experiencing the claustrophobic enclosures of a womb since conception, the atmosphere can play havoc with a

baby's senses. The air is much cooler now that they are stripped off, and it's not nice. As well as wanting to beat my record of 16 seconds for changing a poo-filled nappy, you will probably want to speed up nappy changes to cause as little distress as possible to your baby.

This sensitivity to temperature goes for when your baby is in her cot or basket, too. Apply layers of clothes and bedding rather than heaping all your hopes on a single heavy blanket or duvet. With layers it is much easier to help your baby warm up or cool down ever so slightly.

Cuddles
Babies love being held, and in the early weeks being rocked or swayed is incredibly reminiscent of life in the womb, and will usually result in sleep. Alia and Ronin both seemed particularly happy sleeping on my chest, and on waking would attempt to seek out my nipple (pecks, boy boobs, man tits, call them what you like) for a quick feed...

Babies might weigh less than ten pounds, but until you get used to holding a baby properly, standing up with them for hours can be as exhausting and taxing as a full workout. Use a cushion to support your arm if you have the baby with you on the sofa. It stops you getting a painful ache.

Pain of Birth and Pain in Stomach
Birth is a traumatic experience for both your partner and your baby. Your baby might cry because it simply preferred the peaceful environment of Mummy's tummy to the noisy real world. To use a music analogy, it must be like someone removing you from a room of soft furnishings, incense and polite conversation where you are listening to The Orb, and being unceremoniously dumped in the front row of a Metallica gig.

Colic

Alas, about one in five babies develops colic, which most medical practitioners associate with your baby's digestive tract not quite coping with the sudden introduction of milk. There is no cure for colic, but nor does it have any long-term effects – for your baby. But for the parents it is incredibly hard to hear a baby cry for hours on end, without being able to help. Just rest assured, it does pass.

Too Much Fussing

Ironically, too much fussing, cuddling, nappy changes, kisses and rocking can overstimulate a baby. If this is the case, she will actually be crying because you are doing too much, when really she just wants to be left in her basket staring fixedly at the 100-watt bulb in the lounge. Of course, when a baby is crying, leaving her alone is the last thing you want to do, and therefore it is always the last thing you actually do. When the crying stops, you breathe a collective sigh of relief and after wasting half an hour going through the rest of this list, you wish you had left her a moment longer before charging in with the cavalry. So the two of you promise: next time she starts crying you will leave her for a while to calm down. But all the best-laid plans go to waste, because the moment she starts crying you will repeat the process all over again.

However, no matter how inept and incapable you may feel, don't worry too much: you can always rely on your friendly local midwife to sort out your worries. Don't be shy, talk to your partner's midwife during the early weeks – that's what they're there for.

The Midwife Visits

Stab Him, Stab Him in His Heel...

Thankfully, that farewell wave from the midwives as you

left the hospital, or as they left your home so soon after your baby's birth, wasn't the end of your relationship with the medical establishment. Far from it. You have not really been abandoned, although it may feel like that. In the first few days after your baby is born you will see a midwife at least once, to have a gentle chat and check everything is going well. However, this cosy manner is just a ruse, to put you off guard. Because next time she comes, she's going to be armed. She's going to take the little mite's foot and give it a prick and make him bleed... what can you do? Like most of us, you'll probably cower because someone's doing something important whilst wearing a uniform, and that seems to have the universal effect of making us stay very quiet. Worry not. Apart from the near heart attack that you might suffer, the shocked wail your baby will emit will be over momentarily... and the end does justify the means; here's what the heel-prick test is all about:

Like Bleeding a Stone

Unfortunately for your baby, the midwife is going to want a good blob of blood for this to work. She will puncture hard and won't be satisfied until she notices a 'good bleed'. Be prepared. (Look away if you have to, and cover your baby's eyes whilst you're at it, to spare him any possible trauma the next time you walk past a butcher's window.) It's for the greater good. The blood will be sent off for analysis to test for:

Phenylalanine

Try pronouncing that after a couple of bottles of Newcastle Brown Ale. It's really uncommon, but there are some babies who can't process phenylalanine. Now, what's to become of these poor unfortunate souls? Well, other than a lifetime of misery in the playground should the truth ever get out, the real problem is that it's found in lots of different food products, not least of which is milk. If Baby can't process this, then it really needs to be identified quickly, otherwise that 'boob in the face' snack that is supposed to represent sustenance could lead to serious neurological repercussions.

Big Boy, Is He?
The heel prick is also looking for evidence of the growth hormone – again, it's very rare for there to be any abnormalities in the levels, but only testing will prove one way or another what the truth really is.

Sickle Cell Trait
That single drop of blood is also tested for symptoms of cystic fibrosis, a very dehabilitating disease that needs to be spotted early on. Yes, it's hard to watch a baby not even a week old be subjected to a very modern form of bloodletting, but as you can now see, it's worth it. And at least they're not resorting to leeches, although with NHS budgets reaching meltdown, keep your eyes peeled for midwives trying to sneak a pet tank into your home...

Blood-Sugar Levels
Finally, the heel-prick test is also looking to confirm that your baby can control its blood-sugar level... I very much hope your child passes his first 'test' with distinction.

Bulging Pants!

But are you ready to pass your first test... You've been thinking about changing nappies pretty much constantly since the moment you found out you were going to be a dad. You've been thinking about it because you don't want to do it. You really don't want to do it, ever. To make matters worse, that's all people seem to talk about when they learn you're going to become a father. If you've played it cool thus far, then Mum's already had a few goes at the hospital, and at home you've been under the supervision of the midwife. Chances are, all of the meconium (the evil, treacle-like substance that represents visually and physically all that was ingested during your beautiful baby's experience *in utero*) has been passed and Baby is now excreting something that more closely resembles your own poo, even if it still is a bit of an odd colour. We're certainly moving into familiar territory now, but that doesn't mean you would willingly want to get involved in the clean-up operation...

But you know deep down, don't you, that it's an inevitable part of the fatherhood process. You know that to truly get involved you're going to have to tackle a full nappy, and tackle it you will. My advice is to get on with it as soon as possible. Why? Well, you don't want to run the risk of dealing with this sort of thing all on your own, with your partner out on a jolly or back at work, and you drowning in a sea of baby poo, wee, cotton wool and tears. You're going to need support – not necessarily in the same room, but the knowledge that there's responsible adult back-up in the same house is a massive reassurance should things go horribly wrong. The sooner you get on with it, the more likely you'll get the kudos for 'getting your hands dirty' – quite literally, more often than not – and if you get it spectacularly wrong, then you have the excuse that it's all a bit 'new'... try that one when your baby is more than four weeks old (read: at least 70 nappies changed by your partner) and it really isn't going to leave you in a good light... in fact, you're going to look more like a 40-watt dad flickering on and off in a seedy hotel room.

So, How Do You Do It?
Have everything to hand before you start. Once that dirty

nappy is off (even once the tabs have been loosened) you are committed. For newborns, you want to avoid the pre-packaged wipes and just use cotton wool – spend the extra pennies on the balls, rather than the 'candy floss-sized' economy bag – you don't want to be trying to rip off manageable chunks of cotton wool in the heat of battle; you'll end up using two-thirds of a packet (not to mention having to endure the uncomfortable noise/sensation of ripping cotton wool – I have goose pimples just writing this down...) Have a bowl of warm water to hand, a nappy bag for the soon-to-be-revealed offending article and a suitable surface to change the bum – a changing mat or even a towel will do. Have a new nappy to hand, along with your baby, and open the nappy in advance.

Breathing through your open mouth rather than your nostrils will keep any pungent odours to a minimum and always, always make sure you keep your fingernails either bitten or cut short; you really don't want bits of child poo there.

It's hard, but for those first times, don't worry about trying to do it fast – more haste, less speed; there's a knack, you just need to learn it, Yes, she'll be crying, you'll feel terrible and you'll want to be dealing with the poo as quickly as humanly possible, but you need to get this right. Both boys and girls have a habit of weeing when you're changing their nappy (it's not vindictive, it's a reaction to the sudden change of temperature around their groin), so with baby boys especially, be ready:
a) not to take a golden shower in the face and
b) if he starts to wee, don't be shy about 're-directing' his flow onto the towel or babygro, rather than over your carpets/bed/Turkish rug – a towel is far easier to wash.

Expect sudden movements and jerks, especially once they're a few months old; one minute everything's under control, the next, there's poo all over their foot, your sleeve and the floor.

Nappies – and the Destruction of the Universe

Meanwhile, one of your first major decisions, some would say an almost political decision, is what to do about the poo. For the last 20 years or so disposable nappies have been the preferred choice for parents. Whilst being expensive, they're convenient and a pragmatic solution to the problem. But moods change and there is a strong argument that from an environmental point of view, disposable nappies are pure evil; not only are they a strain on your pocket, they help to destroy the environment in their manufacture and they are a blight on the world in terms of their decomposition. More and more people are going green with their baby's poo... So, what are your options?

Disposable Nappies

Some might say this is the easy, selfish option. They might even be right. Disposable nappies are the standard ones that you can buy from any supermarket or corner shop in the country. Shaped to wrap around Baby's bum and to stick together with minimal-fuss Velcro, disposable nappies are strong, absorbent and comfortable to wear – at least, that's what I understand. I haven't tried wearing one myself recently.

When it comes to dealing with your child's poo, you really want to be shot of the foul stuff as quickly as possible. The disposable nappy facilitates this. Pull off the tabs, remove the offending article, a quick wipe of the bum, a new nappy on, and bingo! You're back in business. Until the next time.

It is a given that disposable nappies are a massive

environmental problem. The reality, for most parents, is that it is better to have a long-term environmental problem than tolerate your child's poo being in the room with you any longer than necessary. It can be an emotive, tricky subject or you can categorically decide from the outset that you couldn't care less and you are going to buy and use disposable nappies right from the off. Either way, you won't be alone. The vast majority of parents use disposable nappies and will continue to do so. Moral and ecological arguments aside, you will choose which nappy route to take very early on, and stick to that decision. Be realistic about how much time you have on any given day and then make your choice.

I don't want to take the moral high ground or the low ground with this book and therefore I have to admit to being a fan of disposable nappies because they suit our circumstances. We do give a damn about the environment, the current state of world peace, poverty, Third-World debt and who shot JR, but we are also realists living in a capitalist society at the turn of the 21st century. We use disposable nappies and will continue to do so until our son is potty-trained. (Roll on the summer!) Our carbon footprint on the world is probably a contributory factor to other people's suffering. For that I am sorry. But my son has got a clean bum and all is well with us. Selfish? Yes, very, but I'm man enough to admit it. If it's any consolation we do our bit by recycling plastics, bottles and tin cans. So should you.

Biodegradable Disposable Nappies
Pretty much the same as above, only you won't be hurting the environment quite so much. There's no pretending that even biodegradable nappies will dissolve away in a matter of days, or even weeks. The reality is that it will take years for the nappies to completely return to the earth. However,

compared to normal nappies, this process is infinitely quicker and therefore if you are any way inclined to think or vote Green, then you should be looking at biodegradable nappies. Despite your fears, biodegradable nappies aren't any less absorbent or in any way inferior to ordinary nappies.

There's an associated cost to biodegradable nappies that you will really notice over the course of your child's early years. That cost may not have an impact on the environment, but it will on your wallet. Availability can also sometimes be an issue if you're not near a supermarket, but there are a number of websites where you can buy biodegradable nappies. *(See Useful Addresses at the back of the book.)* Also be aware that only about 70 per cent of the components in biodegradable nappies actually do degrade quickly; the remaining 30 per cent of materials take hundreds of years, just like regular disposable nappies... Nappies are a blight on the environment. Not just a little bit of a problem but an enormous mountain of non-biodegradable waste that will continue to fester in landfill sites around the world, probably to the end of time. Everyone knows cockroaches will probably be the only survivors of a nuclear holocaust. Used nappies will be their nuclear-winter homes. Sleep well tonight, won't you?

Biodegradable nappies give you a chance to be ethical in your choice of nappies, although not as ethical as with terry nappies. Even taking into account the amount of detergent and electricity and so on used over a three-year period, these are without a doubt the most eco-friendly option. But in reality you can only be as ecologically friendly as your wallet and your schedule allow.

Towel/Terry Nappies – Basic

You probably wore these when you were a lad. Proper nappies. Lengths of towelling wrapped around a baby to catch any and all excretions. This is what people used before disposable nappies ever existed. It's the purists' choice.

Although the initial outlay is quite high because it's recommended that you have at least two dozen, once you've bought them, that's it. You will never run out of nappies and you will never have to buy any more. In a nutshell, you'll save about £700 a year, per baby, for two to three years. That's about £2,000 for just one child, or a 42-inch HD-ready plasma-screen television.

You have to learn nappy origami in order to convert that square of terry cloth into something wearable, and you're always at risk of spiking your son and daughter with a giant safety pin. Oh, and there's the poo. Lots of poo. Lots of washing too. If you didn't have enough on your plate already, you'll be adding the rather unfortunate daily grind of removing poo and washing heavily-soiled nappies. It's not going to make your life any easier. Or much more fun. Thankfully, you can invest in nappy liners, which mean that you can pick up the poo in the removable lining and flush it all away down the loo – far easier and far less messy.

It's decision time. Both the environmental and the financial arguments are obviously in favour of using towel nappies, but the reality of being cash-rich, time-poor wage slaves is that most of us choose to stick two fingers up at the world and plunge a whole fist into our pockets to keep life simple, convenient and 'more hygienic'. I would very much like to pretend that I fought the good fight and continue to happily scrub my child's nappies until my knuckles are raw. The truth is, I took the easy option and continue to buy disposable nappies to this day. Be realistic about how much effort is required and make your decision accordingly.

Towel/Terry Nappies – Advanced

Fortunately, technology has advanced since the days when you were bundled up in your terry cloth. Enjoy the environmental and cash benefits of 'real' nappies with the new models – designed to resemble their disposable cousins, and just as straightforward to use. Nice.

With a plethora of groovy, Velcro-fastened numbers to choose from, shopping for nappies has never been this exciting! You will be able to choose nappies with printed patterns, or just keep it plain. Some have plastic covers, some not. Some come with disposable liners that you just flush down the loo with the poo. The manufacturers really are making it easier to be environmentally aware – it just boils down to whether you want to take that step or not.

Just as with the original terries there is going to be more washing required and a regular interaction between your hand and your child's poo, but just think of all the money you'll save. A strong argument for cloth nappies is that Baby can feel when they're wet/dirty, and he lets you know about it. That helps with potty training later on. If you've got the cash there are companies who wash the nappies for you and deliver them back smelling sweet as roses. Environmentally friendly *and* hassle-free. That's what we like.

Come Swim With Me

And then there's the bath. Bathing a child for the first time is absolutely terrifying. Never in a million years would you want to expose your little baby to a body of water so vast, so deep and so full of danger that your heart races at the mere mention of the words 'bath time' and yet, deep down, you know the time has come to clean the poor little mite. His skin has been flaking since the day he was born; he's excreted all manner of liquids and solids from every bodily orifice all in a matter of the past few hours; his hair is still slightly matted in maternal blood and the lump of dead flesh previously known as the umbilical cord has not only withered and blackened, but is most definitely beginning to pong...

On goes the hot tap and on goes the cold – how warm is 'warm' to a couple-of-days-old baby? Would he appreciate soothing bath salts? Relaxing herbal aromas? A bath bomb? You don't want to scald him and you don't want to make him shiver with the sinister vibrations you inflicted earlier whilst trying to change his nappy... Baths should be relaxing. Baths should be fun. What's so difficult?

Well, for a start, if supporting the weight of a baby (the phrase, 'eight pounds two ounces, my arse,' springs to mind again) at arm's length over a potentially fatal body of water, isn't enough to make you think twice, then the sudden realization that you are using both hands to hold your baby and can't possibly reach the shampoo/ bubbles/soap/flannel/towel to help you actually clean and dry the baby will leave you wondering why any parent would ever consider such a ridiculously dangerous task. But it is possible. As with everything to do with fatherhood, it'll come to you. And once you've mastered the basics, it all becomes a lot more rewarding.

What's the Most Rewarding Part of Being a Dad?

Mark: *That's a very long list. I just really enjoy my son's company.*

Richard: *Seeing their pride and happiness when they achieve something that matters to them.*

Paul: *Just one smile a day and I am a happy man...*

Owen: *Oh, that smile...*

Zazz: *India's giggles and Luka's chuckles.*

Mark: *I can be almost comatose from a day full of whatever it is I'm supposed to do at work, but the moment I open the front door at home and the two of them run up to me demanding entertainment, the fun starts.*

Rhys: *Getting to watch daytime TV... and mixing with M.I.L.F.s*

Chapter Three

The Mother

Your partner is a heroine. A fighter. You've seen a side to her – both during the pregnancy and especially during the birth – that has you occasionally questioning your 'manhood'. She's tough, she's resilient, she's able to call upon reserves of energy you didn't know existed and she's still the beautiful, sassy, feminine fox you fell in love with all those years ago... But she is going to need your help now... The question is: are you man enough?

Milk Machine

It's lucky that one of you knows what's going on with this baby business. And it's even luckier that that person isn't you. Babies like to feed. A lot. In fact they like to feed about once every four hours, night and day. When they're first born, this can be as often as every two hours. It's kind of cute during the day – oh look, my partner has her waps out, again! But as the hours pass, and you both become more familiar with four in the morning, the novelty wears off. Babies need to be fed – but how? Although, of course, the final decision rests with your partner, it would really be most responsible for you to encourage her to breastfeed. However, do expect a counter-argument from her, along the lines of: 'It's all very well you wanting me to breastfeed, but you try having a baby latched to your tit for eight hours a day and you'd soon be dashing off to the shops for some formula.'

OK, she's right, we can't possibly know how hard it is, at first. But it's natural, it's supposed to work... And don't for a moment start to ponder on your own neuroses about it interfering with your sex life (your baby has done that already, just by existing), or give a thought to the supposed connection between breastfeeding and 'saggy' tits. Breastfeeding is what breasts are for: food for your baby. Breastfeeding is simply the all-round better option. Here's why:

Breastfeeding

Research shows, beyond doubt, that breastfeeding is better for your baby. However, in the UK we as a nation are pretty rubbish at sticking to breastfeeding, with more than a third of mums opting for formula without even trying breastfeeding. And for those who do start breastfeeding, only 40 per cent are still feeding six weeks later.

And that's really not good. Breastfeeding is essentially your baby's first vaccination (without the need for a needle); Mum's antibodies are transferred via the milk and can protect Baby against a wide range of bacterial, viral, fungal and parasitic infections. And you can forget your fancy yoghurts with friendly bacteria – breast milk enables Baby's gut to develop its own friendly bacteria.

Cholesterol, despite what the Carol Vorderman adverts tell us, is not all bad. Lashings and lashings of the good type can be found in breast milk – it's there to help neural development by promoting growth of 'cable insulation' of the nerve fibres. Helping turn Baby into a toned, strong, temple of an athlete (just like Dad...). Cholesterol also promotes enzymes which (ironically) will help break down cholesterol in later life. And all this, for free. I hate to be political, but with a wife who's a midwife and friends who spend their spare time as breastfeeding counsellors (and knowing they will read this!), I'm happy to be an advocate for it. And us mere 'blokes' might have more influence on the breast/formula argument than might at first appear... And we do like to have some hard facts.

Statistics show that bottle-fed babies are more likely to end up being hospitalized due to diarrhoea and respiratory problems. They're also more likely to suffer from wheezes, ear infections, urinary-tract infections and eczema, amongst other complaints. Children who were bottle-fed are also more likely to end up being obese and developing diabetes. Shocking, isn't it? Breastfeeding also helps protect mums from breast cancer, ovarian cancer and, later on in life, hip fractures. It can also help her return to pre-pregnancy weight. Not only that, but it costs at least £450 a year for artificial milk! Free, if you're breastfeeding.

Supporting Your Partner

If you want what's best for your baby, you'll have to work hard to support your partner, particularly in the first six weeks while breastfeeding is becoming established. Yes, it takes up to six weeks, but it's well worth it in the end. For a start, you will avoid the complication of having to prepare bottles in the middle of the night. Also when you go out, breast milk is always at the ideal serving temperature, whereas you have to find somewhere to warm up formula milk.

So if she does want to try breastfeeding, a few days after the birth your partner's body will gear up and start producing milk. This can be quite sudden to begin with, and what is termed 'engorgement' takes place. Sounds quite pornographic, I know, and it does lead, very quickly, to enormous breasts, which, sadly, you will not be allowed anywhere near. Engorgement can be quite uncomfortable but there are things you can do to help. Warmth will be soothing – run your partner a bath and insist that she has a good soak – and be a love and get some warm gel pads from the chemist. Understand that your partner may need to express a little milk prior to feeding, as a newborn mouth may have trouble getting to grips with such enormous melons! Be on hand to apply a cool pad after feeds – it's soothing. If you're feeling cheap, or want to be quite natural about these sorts of things, get the missus to try cold cabbage leaves – bliss for her, but a tad smelly!

Don't make any demands, but constantly find subtle opportunities to mention that natural feeding is best for Baby – particularly when they're tiny. Babies don't know when it's day or night, and aren't interested in the fact that you need to go to the supermarket, or are on the telephone. They want to feed when they're hungry. Don't get a guilt complex – when her milk first comes in (during the first week) and her boobs are aching, desperate to release their warm payload, there's nothing wrong with waking up the baby and encouraging a feed. With a full tummy, he'll soon be back in the land of nod – as will your partner; as will you.

If breastfeeding hurts like hell, or is causing blisters, or cracked nipples are raging in your household, it's time to call in the professionals: a breast-feeding counsellor should be top of the list (and your job is to *nip* down to the chemist in search of *nipple* cream). Really! Breastfeeding should be without pain. It's important to remember that generally, after six weeks, breastfeeding becomes much easier as Baby settles into more of a pattern. Easy for us blokes to say, granted, but it's true!

Research shows, categorically, that breastfeeding within the first hour after birth is important to establish a good feeding pattern. I know you've just watched her give birth, and could understand if she said she wasn't really in the mood for some mouth-on-tit action... but this might take some of your famous *persuasion* tactics. Also, skin-to-skin contact is intrinsically linked to long-term breastfeeding, so again this should be something you should champion.

An astonishing quarter of your partner's entire calorie expenditure will be used on feeding your child; so make sure she gets plenty of rest, and eats and drinks well. Healthy stuff, mind, not your pot noodle and bacon avec lard surprise! Don't be surprised if Baby feeds every one to two hours in the first few weeks. Baby's tummy is very small – the size of a walnut, in fact. Breast milk is easily digested and is processed very rapidly. Unlike formula, which is like having a Christmas dinner every time – sounds good, but you know it's bad for you! Understandably, formula-fed babies will often sleep longer between feeds (just to avoid the equivalent of their 17th mince pie for the day); so would you in a similar situation. And growth spurts can make the frequency of feeds go up again. (Bear in mind that as a percentage of overall height, a 2mm growth spurt is pretty significant – you try adding an extra three inches to your height, overnight, powered by nothing more substantial than a couple of litres of blue top.)

If during the early evening Baby is constantly at

the breast, you need to check that your partner is getting enough food/drink/rest mid-afternoon. If Mum's feeling like she isn't producing enough milk, she probably *is*. It's just that Baby wants to feed frequently. Funnily enough, this helps promote supply – her breasts will soon catch up with demand. Mum can express milk for ten minutes each side following feeds to stimulate supply. Store it in the fridge next to the Chardonnay – and be sure to use within 24 hours or freeze it for later use.

Get Mum and Baby to rest up for a few days. If possible, and you're still on paternity leave, put Mum to bed, with Baby in the Moses basket. Just having your baby in the same room will stimulate her milk supply, as will getting as much rest as possible. Evidence suggests that letting your baby share your room for the first six months is advisable – it will encourage breastfeeding and acts as a form of protection against cot death.

Encourage Mum to try different feeding positions. Lying down is the one to master – it's much more comfortable for night feeds. It's preferable to put Baby back in the Moses basket afterwards due to the risk of squashing Baby or overheating under duvet. However, guidance to reduce risk of accidents is:

How to Reduce the Risk of Cot Death

- Do not share bed with Baby if you smoke, or if you have had a drink, or are unusually tired. (So, another night on the sofa for you, my man.)
- Undress Baby to the same number of layers you wear in bed.
- Don't let covers go over Baby's head.
- No pets in or on the bed, day or night.
- Never let your baby sleep on a sofa due to risk of overheating or getting wedged between cushions.

Soon Mum will master the art and be able to feed discretely in restaurants and so on, and woe betide anyone who berates her or wants to send her off to the WC to feed. Would you eat your dinner in a toilet? It's illegal in Scotland to tell people to move on for breastfeeding! But elsewhere in the UK police have been summoned over complaints about women breastfeeding. Ridiculous!!! Fight the good fight. And if you need any more excuses, from a purely selfish, male point of view, your life will be whole lot easier if she breastfeeds. Simple as that. Needless to say, however, come the time she decides to stop feeding, for whatever reason, you must back her up 100 per cent. Even if she decides she wants to bottle-feed from the outset.

Express Yourself...

We're 'hands-on' dads, that's why you're reading this book and that's why you helped with Baby's bath tonight. But as much as we might want to, we can't lactate. However, where's there's a will, there's a way and you too can be involved in feeding your baby. You, or more accurately, your partner, may want to use a breast pump (either manual or electric; ask the midwife/breast councillor if they are available to hire in your area; if not, you'll have to buy one) so that she can express milk. Which can either be kept in the fridge (if it is to be used within the next 24 hours) or frozen, for up to three months, in bags or containers that you can store next to the fish fingers and the corn on the cob portions.

Empowerment! You have the still-warm milk, you have your sterilized (but now cooled-down) bottle and teat, and you're away, insta-boob. Why is the act of feeding a baby so special? I'm guessing it's got a lot to do with simple psychology. We want to feed people we love and care for – to keep them alive, to share the hunt, to celebrate life together. So sneak off to a corner, bring the bottle, your child, some muslin sheets (and a cushion for your arm) and get feeding!

I should add, in addition to the above, that the latest research by lactation consultants is that it's now best *not* to use teats very early on in your newborn's life as they may confuse baby – possibly leading to baby rejecting your partner's nipple. The alternative? Use a small sterile cup, such as an egg cup (preferably one without a hole in the bottom!), and your baby will use her tongue and lap the milk, just like a cat. It's up to the two of you to do what you think best.

A word of warning – your partner may get on well with breastfeeding but that doesn't necessarily mean that she'll find expressing easy, or worthwhile. A baby sucking her boob causes a number of emotional and physiological effects. Sticking her breast into a cold plastic contraption is not the same, and expressing can be a long, arduous and sometimes painful experience. Add the fact that the pump and all the other paraphernalia then need to be dismantled, sterilized and put back together, all for 10ml of milk, and you'll begin to understand, if not share, her dismay at the very thought of expressing.

This could leave you high and dry in the feeding stakes, but at the end of the day, you still have plenty of time together to enjoy one another. Feeding isn't the be-all and end-all. Take Baby out for a walk while Mum has a bath. Come home half an hour earlier from work when you can – Mum will be eternally grateful. Make bath time or the story before bed 'dad time'. Being stuck indoors with a baby permanently attached to your boob, watching *Ready Steady Cook* and *Countdown*, is enough eventually to send most post-baby hormonal mums into a state of despair. I became a big fan of *Judge Judy* during my tenure as Mr Mum; I'm not sure why. But it was the only thing on. And what's more worrying, I probably now know more about American small claims court proceedings than I do about the UK system...

Sore Nipples

My wife was adamant (stand and deliver!) she was going to breastfeed, and it was all going so well until she experienced the curse of the sore nipples. She persevered and it paid off, but problems with feeding can be extremely difficult for Mum, Baby and for Dad, who must stand back and observe this most difficult of times – especially because we're dying to get in there ourselves and feed our progeny, the only way we can, with a bottle.

Sore nipples are caused by any combination of factors. First, and especially with a first baby, up until now they have not been used to feed babies, and that can come as quite a shock to the system – even though this was exactly the task for which breasts and nipples were designed (although I'm sure you have your own strong views on this). Another reason may be poor positioning. A good feeding technique should ensure that the nipple should not have turned white through compression when it comes out, nor should it be flattened. If it is, Mum will soon feel sore. Sore nipples can appear chapped and crusty and in some cases even begin to bleed. To put the pain that this causes into some perspective, my wife declared that it would be easier to give birth ten times over than experience sore nipples again. The fix – well, for many women it's the humble nipple cream, which is obviously safe for Baby to ingest. The important thing, from your perspective, is to remain positive and support your partner's decision to breastfeed. If she's obviously suffering and struggling, then suggest a consultation with her midwife. Find out about local breastfeeding support groups – they will help check that she's positioning Baby well, and the support and encouragement they provide may give her the strength needed to carry on.

Mastitis
If breastfeeding really does become problematic, then do look out for flu-like symptoms, a high temperature, or a sudden increase in your partner's complaints about how sore her boobs are, especially if either of you notices any reddened patches. All of these symptoms may indicate mastitis – which is basically the medical term for blocked ducts. This is not something that can be 'ridden' through. Make sure she contacts her midwife or GP. She's probably not going to feel like it, but it's really important to continue to feed through sore breasts as this will help empty the milk ducts and the alveoli. Encourage different breastfeeding positions to drain all the ducts, such as lying down, or holding Baby underarm like a rugby ball when feeding. But be warned – some GPs still advise women to give up breastfeeding when they have mastitis and are taking antibiotics. Be sure she consults her midwife first.

Giving up
Only your partner can decide when to give up breastfeeding, if she feels it's not working out. Mums can feel overwhelmingly guilty – take care not to add to that. If it's possible, suggest she talk it through with a breastfeeding counsellor first, as some minor changes to the position may help. You've done your job, and now it's important to support her decision (and mean it). There is no 'normal' length of time for breastfeeding; more often than not Baby will lose interest, especially when there are exciting solids or semi-solids on offer. Or your partner's work commitments may play a role, or you may reach the stage where friends begin to give you both funny looks as your 18-year-old son starts rummaging in his mum's bra for

a pre-pub snack! The decision to stop feeding can be both emotive and scary for a new mum – it's your job to facilitate a smooth transition and to look out for her emotional wellbeing whatever her decision.

Her Baby Blues

When the florist finally stops his daily trip to your house with *yet another* delivery of flowers, alarm bells should start ringing in your head. (I'm assuming that you remembered to add to the abundance of fragrant foliage yourself.) Those alarm bells should be warning you to be extra vigilant now and to be extra-sensitive to your partner's needs, requirements and general wellbeing. About a week after the birth of your child, the hormones that have been flying around your partner's body for the entire length of the pregnancy suddenly stop being produced. The net effect of this is that her body crashes. After nine months of hormone-fuelled pregnancy, the total-body experience that is birth and the absolute ecstasy of becoming a mum, your partner is now being forced to detox and is suffering cold turkey. As with dependency on illicit (or prescribed) substances, the withdrawal effects can be incredibly powerful and may leave your partner feeling absolutely terrible.

What is difficult for us dads to understand is how anyone can feel depressed when there is a beautiful baby sharing your lives. If we're honest, despite a few disrupted nights sleep, we're feeling better about life than we have in quite a few years. But the reality for your partner is that she will feel pretty poo for a while. While this is entirely natural, it can be difficult to understand. How can someone who always appeared to be so bubbly, so excited about life, and who seems to have so much going for them (not to mention being the mum to a beautiful little baby) possibly feel depressed? Well, it happens, and it is incredibly common. What we are all (including many mums) guilty of overlooking is that although pregnancy and birth may well be natural, it doesn't necessarily *come naturally*. Giving birth to a child, getting to grips with feeding and simply the overwhelming realization that you are now a *mother* can be overpowering and disorienting. Yes, there are medical staff on hand to look after the physical wellbeing of Mum and child, but what about the emotional side? If the birth has had such a profound effect on us blokes, can we even begin to imagine what's going on in our partner's head? Even with you on hand to help, the whole thing can remain overwhelming for your partner.

No matter how strong you think your partner is, no matter how well-equipped she may seem in terms of her confidence and ability to cope, there is simply no telling as to whether or not she might suffer from the baby blues or, even worse, post-natal depression. It is beyond her control.

Happy Mum, Sad Mum – the Baby Blues or Post-Natal Depression?

Right after the birth, you will both feel a great sense of achievement and pride. The euphoria of becoming parents is a pretty powerful force. For the first three or four days all you can do is grin and run around the place ensuring that absolutely everything is just right for your baby. The house has never been tidier – certainly not when you've had anything to do with it anyway. Already your baby is a matter of days old, rather than a matter than hours. Visitors are still knocking on the door and flowers are still arriving (not necessarily the case if this is your second or third child; everyone is getting a bit bored with your ability to procreate at this stage). You're hopefully already (or will be very soon) a master of the nappy change and you laugh back to the time when you thought that bathing a baby was a much more difficult procedure than open-heart surgery, and as you were unqualified, one you didn't want to be involved in either. You have both managed an hour or so sleep a night and yet remain feeling pretty good. (The novelty of sleepless nights will soon wear off.) But all good things come to an end and before the week is out, your partner may well go full-circle and become a weeping wreck. This is unlikely to be post-natal depression, but probably is what is known as the 'baby blues'. They are not tears of joy, as I mistakenly assumed, but tears of sadness. 'But you have a beautiful baby in your arms,' you might well ask. 'What possible reasons have you got to cry?' Lots and lots it seems.

In part, this sudden drop in the happiness scale will be your partner fully relaxing after the whirlwind of the previous few days. She won't have fully recovered from the labour and birth, and it has been pure adrenalin and love of the new baby that has given her the strength, and will, to keep going. When exhaustion catches up, not to mention the sudden lack of hormones mentioned above, it will poleaxe your partner and it is not a pleasant sight.

Worry not. The 'baby blues' are, for most women, temporary. They will probably consist of a few days of fear about their ability, their 'right', and even their suitability, to be a mother. As far as you will be concerned, from what you've seen so far your partner is possibly the most capable mother on the planet. She didn't feel awkward about changing nappies or feeding the baby, whereas you did. How can she be questioning her ability? No one else is – not even *your* own mother! But sometimes the baby blues do not disappear after a few days; sometimes they're here to stay for a while. And in extreme cases they can develop into post-natal depression.

Not to make light of it, but I find the best way to

understand post-natal depression is to remember back to when you first learnt that your partner was pregnant. Mixed in with the euphoria was a heap load of stress; for days, weeks or even the whole nine months, you had post-positive test result depression. All those worries about your job, money, time and ability to cope hit you nine months before they did your partner. You've recovered, and now the baby is there in the flesh and you're just getting on with it all. For your partner, however, those fears are very much *in the now* and more importantly, are magnified 100 times over.

For about one in every ten mothers, the feelings of inadequacy and inability to cope will last longer than a few days. Days can become weeks and even months. Post-natal depression is an illness, and fortunately it can be treated. But first it must be diagnosed. There are some telltale symptoms of both the baby blues and post-natal depression and it is important for you to be on the lookout for:

Depression
This is the most common symptom and I suppose the most obvious. Your partner will be feeling very low about herself and even about being a mother. Often the depression comes in phases, possibly triggered at certain times of the day, but sometimes completely unpredictable. Sufferers describe it as an intense sadness: feeling utterly miserable and incredibly lonely, even though they have a small baby constantly by their side. Your partner may be unwilling to make commitments too far in advance (like next Tuesday), and can seem very isolated from friends, other mothers and even you!

Fatigue
You will have become used to seeing your partner

exhausted from about the start of the third trimester. You are also pretty tired now, what with all the night-time feeds, nappy changes and crying. There's also the small matter of somehow trying to concentrate on a full-time career, but I wouldn't advise complaining too much about that, as it is likely your partner is envious of your freedom to leave the house and the baby every day. But your partner will be fatigued from the constant attention she is giving the baby, all day and all night, not to mention the physical drain if she is breastfeeding. All of these factors are taking their toll. Coupled with the fatigue come:

Inability to sleep
So tired that she nods off with the baby for five minutes on the sofa, but equally too tired to sleep properly in a bed, your partner may be feeling so depressed or worried about your baby that even though she wants and needs nothing more than a good rest, she cannot get to sleep.

Irritability
The telltale sign for most dads that there may be something wrong with your partner is an intense irritability. Ironically, you may well be the focus of it and left wondering what you said or did wrong. Your partner may also be irritated with the baby, or getting to grips with breastfeeding (which can be extremely uncomfortable to establish, and should not be underestimated as a potential problem). Unfortunately it is likely to be you, or even other children in the house, who bear the brunt of her irritability.

Up and Down Appetite
Her body is craving nutrients and calories to help her recover from the birth, and if she is breastfeeding, to keep your baby healthy. But she might hardly eat anything at all, or, just as bad, start eating lots of the wrong things. You

might not be able to influence a lot of what gets eaten, or not eaten, during the day, but as with the latter part of pregnancy, it might be time to release the inner chef in you in time for the evening meal. Delicious and nutritious dad scran is the order of the day.

Can't Cope, Won't Cope
Your partner might start complaining that it is all too much, or start to break down on the telephone to you, her family or her friends, about the demands of the baby. She is anxious that the baby is not developing properly or that she is an unfit mother. The care of the baby is a chore, and an unwelcome one at that. The baby is never satisfied and/or ungrateful for her efforts.

Or perhaps your partner becomes overly concerned about your baby's health and runs to the doctor almost daily. Is the baby getting enough milk; is he getting too much? Molehills have become mountains, and you're being shouted at for not worrying enough...

No One Is Immune
Regardless of your partner's previous mental disposition, the baby blues and post-natal depression can affect even the 'strongest' women. They can, of course, also affect women who already have children. These feelings will eventually go, but recognizing them quickly and getting your partner to acknowledge them could save you both months, maybe even years, of suffering, not to mention the unwelcome strain on your relationship as a couple.

How Can You Help?

So where does that leave us blokes? Well, it means that you will be required to continue with some of the duties that you may have assumed towards the latter weeks of the pregnancy. If you want your partner to come through this, quite simply you will need to remove as many of the burdens from her day as you possibly can – but also not infringe too much on your partner forming a relationship with your new baby. This can be a difficult balance to achieve as your partner's needs (and your intervention) will be unique – no two relationships are the same and no two women will suffer from the baby blues in exactly the same way.

In a strange paradox, your role will be to maximize the time your partner can spend with your baby, whilst at the same time looking closely for opportunities where it would really help if your partner could have some time to herself – if only to get a few hours of uninterrupted sleep. How does this work in reality? Well, it involves not treating every day as routine. Whilst you might well have a job that involves deadlines and a routine way of looking at every second Tuesday, your partner's appreciation of the days of the week has probably altered drastically. In the same way that you might dread every second Thursday, because it involves reporting to management, your partner may dread the coming of every single day because she does not know *what* is going to occur. This ambiguity is quite exciting at first, but quickly turns to chaos. There are no rules. One day everything is within arm's reach and she feels accomplished. The next day nothing particular has altered, and yet everything becomes an insurmountable hurdle. This same woman, a matter of months ago, was closing multi-million pound deals, speaking fluent Japanese and leaving you for dead in the salary battle. This morning, she couldn't put on a pair of socks without collapsing in a flood of tears because you left the toilet seat up...

What Can You Do?
Support, Support, Support. Yes, you might well be feeling

that you are in need of some support yourself, what with the new baby on the scene. You have suddenly become second in line in your partner's feelings and affections, and thus far it has been a very slow-moving line. But getting in a huff about being demoted from favourite to second-best is really not going to help the situation. You know your partner best and that familiarity will be more effective in helping her with her baby blues than most medications or third-party advice.

All that said, if you feel the situation is beyond your control, your partner or you might feel that outside help is also required. In this case please do visit your local GP, or use the contact details which are provided at the end of the book.

Your Baby Blues

No matter how much you think you are prepared for a child, until he's actually there, clothed in the babygros you've been buying over the last couple of months, gurgling, puking and filling nappies, it's not real. My main problem, which I apparently shared with many of the men interviewed, is that I was all geared up to deal with the pregnancy and prepare for the birth as best I could and I somehow believed that it all ended there. Even though we know it's all leading up to a baby being born, we still kind of cling to the hope that our baby will be sentient, fully conversant, and ready for a quick game of Monopoly the moment they are born. We don't let our minds wander too far into the future and, to be honest, when the future suddenly is *now* we're at a loss as to what to do next, just as we were when we first learnt that our partner was pregnant. Back to square one, then.

The reality of life with a newborn can hit us hard, usually about a week after the birth and, unfortunately enough, just at the time that your partner is beginning to suffer from the baby blues herself. So here the two of you are, moping around the place, both desperate for a full night's sleep, not able to understand why you're not feeling quite as happy as you should be. She's struggling to put in her earrings and you're struggling to comprehend the reality of life. All too recently you were a carefree, single, live-by-your-own-rules kind of guy. Suddenly, here you are in a room with a baby and a partner bordering on depression. How, exactly, did this all happen? Deep down you know you wanted it, but now she's here, now there is a living, breathing child in the cot at the bottom of the bed, it all takes on a new slant. Surprised? I certainly was.

Chapter Four

Becoming a Dad

'Right, Off You Pop.'

Hey? You want her to leave? But we've just got here! Does no one else here realize that this woman has just given birth? To a baby! I got three days in hospital to recover from an appendectomy... the rather straightforward procedure of removing the appendix. Surely, in acknowledgement and celebration of the fact that this woman, my partner, has brought a new life into the world, vaginally or otherwise, she deserves a bit more time to recover? But no. The medical staff wants you out (usually within 48 hours) because they need to fill the bed with someone else. Simple as that. You have extended your family and that extended family is taking up too much room.

Apart from a few visits from a midwife and then a few more from a health visitor, unless you or your baby has the misfortune to suffer an emergency, that's pretty much the end of your contact with medical professionals for quite a while. This abandonment can feel quite profound and the next few weeks will be challenging, but never lose sight of how daunting it is for your partner too (although women do often seem to have the ability to appear so calm and at ease with this sudden promotion into parenthood, you might question whether they've actually secretly done it all before). So let's get down to the real nitty-gritty. No one likes housework, so why should it be your partner's job? Start now, make sure that house is looking tip-top for your baby's arrival. Think how many photos are going to be taken in your house over the coming weeks; we don't want telltale crumbs on the carpet caught on film and kept forever in photo albums across the country, do we? The Hoover's probably under the stairs if you're wondering.

Be Prepared?

Do any of us feel prepared for fatherhood? I certainly didn't. I still don't. It's fair to say I'm still learning. Did my panel of experts feel prepared?

Mark: *I probably did think I was prepared at the time, but now I know I had no idea what it's like. But I suppose I was ready in many ways – financially stable, that bit older and a homeowner.*

Richard: *Not really. Not sure how you can be.*

Rhys: *I can't say I was prepared but I've always been pretty relaxed about stuff and always related well to children and babies. I certainly don't remember feeling anxious about it.*

Paul: *Not even slightly prepared; without the classes I would have been sunk. We invested in the NCT classes; these were not only excellent in preparing us mentally for having a baby but also got us a circle of five other couples, and we have met up every week since...*

Owen: *No. Is anyone prepared for the first time? New territory.*

Zazz: *No, I didn't have a clue.*

Chris: *I still don't feel adequately prepared. Every day is a school day. When they're pregnant you think of things in the future that you know and can associate with, such as teaching them to ride a bike or playing football. I had no idea the body temperature that a baby shouldn't exceed or what was causing the cradle cap on my boy's head.*

Mark: *No. I still don't feel adequately prepared for being a father. It's one of those things that could terrify you if you ever sat down and analyzed the responsibility that you've been given. Fortunately you never get the time to analyze, or sit down, when you've got kids.*

Left for the Very First Time

It was going to happen sooner or later. You did your best to stall her and to make a million excuses as to why it was much more prudent for *you* to just nip down to the shops to get whatever it was you forgot last time. But this is really it. She's going out without the baby! To press the point any more will make it all too obvious that you're scared stiff and can't handle the pressure. And now is not a good time to be showing weakness and a lack of moral fibre. Granted you've read the guidebooks and seen your partner in action, but that is absolutely no substitute for having to deal with the situation on your own. Ground, swallow me up now, I am not able to cope!

It's sod's law: the moment your partner leaves the house your baby will cry. At any other time you can come and go as you please, banging doors, breaking plates and generally making a nuisance of yourself, and your baby will sleep. But the moment, nay, the nanosecond, that your partner blows you a kiss and closes the door quietly, your baby will know. So the door clicks shut and you hear a whimper. For the last five days straight your child has been asleep at four o'clock, but not today. Because Mummy has gone out he is going to play up and this is your baptism of fire. Thankfully your partner, especially if she is breastfeeding, will not want to be away for long, but even 20 minutes will feel like a lifetime. What on earth are you going to do? If anything bad *can* happen, it *will* happen on your watch. You know it already. And then it does.

Keep calm. This is nothing you cannot handle. Your heart will feel the worse for wear, but you'll manage. Don't try to do anything fancy, like try to deal with the baby and prepare a three-course meal. Put everything else on hold. Your project, until the missus is back in the house, is your baby. Nothing else. Surely it can't be *that* difficult...?

Well, on that note, and with tongue very much in cheek, I would like to present to you the Bloke's Guide to Baby Targets and Parental Guidelines.

The Bloke's Guide to Baby Timetables – What to Expect, Apparently...

Preparations for Day One
Have you locked your pit-bull attack dog in the garage? Have you stuck your collection of razor-sharp Samurai swords in the shed? Have you put up the Mamas & Papas

cot? You had better, mate, because soon you are going to have to go off down the hospital and pick up your missus and your baby – and don't forget the car seat...

What Will Life Be Like, Month One?

Well, babies are absolutely tiny and look like wrinkled old men. Their cry is a bit weird, sort of, 'Whaaa! Whaaa!' and it's bloody scary. Most books tell you that at this stage of the baby's life, the baby will sleep a lot and suck its thumb. That's all true, but what should concern you is that you are going to have to learn to change the nappy of a tiny Homo sapien and it is really tricky when it contains a small thing that wriggles. Expect to get woken up in the middle of the night. Expect to learn how to feed it. Expect not to go to the pub.

If the grandparents can get their digital cameras far enough away from the new baby for you to see him, he might be able to see you too – providing you are only about 30cm (a foot) away. As time moves on, he will be able to recognize your frightened-little-boy look from a metre (three feet) away. He will also be able to smell you (not pleasant), the same way a newborn can smell where its mum has gone and where its breast milk is at. By the end of the first month he will begin to learn to smile. Are you feeling emotional yet? (Don't worry if you don't feel too attached at first, that's quite normal too.)

By the end of the month you can relax a little as the baby is a bit more robust. You still can't drop him or knock him off the sofa, but the good news is that his head is less wobbly now, which is a huge relief for new dads. Don't get complacent; you still have to be very careful with him.

From One to Three Months – the Truth

Right, you are still getting no sleep. You have probably only managed to get to the pub once, that time when you lied about being late back from going to the supermarket, and you are probably back at work now and so a bit of a sleep-deprived office moron. Your baby will have been carted off to the local Registry Office by now and given some name, which you liked at the time, and you are beginning to get into the feeding regime. You will have had no sex whatsoever and if you smoke, you'd better keep a clean t-shirt and canister of deodorant in your car (pregnant and breastfeeding women develop a sense of smell to rival Spiderman's).

The good news is that your baby is beginning to look a bit more normal and to toughen up. They make gurgling and other baby noises and don't panic and do that strange star-jump reflex thing every time you make a loud noise. (Although a proper bloke-tastic sneeze provokes a reaction worth trying to catch on camera – not to be cruel, but it really is hilarious. For us, not necessarily for your baby...) They now know you are the noisy one who knocks things over and that your wife is the nice quiet one who smells of milk rather than sweat and stress. They are even trying to move (ah, bless). They can also see better and seem to have got the hang of the old wobbly-head business. They can also grip stuff, like your finger and coat and hair, and mobile phone – so watch out.

From Three to Six Months – the Truth
There is a chance by now that your wife/partner may just be willing to give you a shag or at least offer the compromise of a quick hand-job. Your ability to think of lies to get you out of the housework and, circumstances willing, to engage grandparents to come over and cover, err... sorry, help out, will have improved dramatically. By now you should be able to change a dirty nappy at high speed, know various forms of creams and food (by brand name) and be fit to be left alone with the baby

for an hour without having to call Social Services and the SAS for help. Your fatherhood credentials have, hopefully, been well established.

As for your baby, well they're quite interesting now. For a start they are often very big and cute, and not unlike a puppy, and, in a crude sense, they can also be entertaining. They often roll back and forth, they will start to lift themselves up and learn to crawl. Feel free to support them as you pretend that they can walk, when they can't (don't drop them, though). Overall they are much better coordinated and easier to deal with. Supposedly they cry less, but they still can't talk yet. Oh, and they should be easier to feed. It is highly likely that you will have loads of your partner's female mates hanging round at this time and lots of visits from the in-laws.

From Six to Nine Months – the Truth
Up to the age of nine months, babies exhibit actions that are similar to yours when you are completely pissed out of your head. They will try to sit up by themselves, at first with difficulty. They will try to crawl about the floor, again with difficulty, and they will try to hold themselves up using the furniture. Although not in complete control of their actions, they can reach for things that are placed down for them (like your doner kebab). They will start to be able to grip stuff tightly and remember things, but they may also develop a fear of strangers, which is a great excuse for running away from adoring neighbours or people in the supermarket, or odd family members, depending on your own personal views...

From Nine to Twelve Months – the Truth
Welcome to the realm of competitive parents. You may not like it in yourself, but from now on you will secretly, or overtly, compare your child to others. By now you will

either be patting yourself on the back in the secure knowledge that your child is a genius, or you will be working out how much that Montessori school might cost in the depressed hope that they will be able to coach your beloved baby into learning sufficient skills for them to work part-time at Lidl. This is truly stupid because, basically, babies develop at different speeds, but believe you me, you will still be hooked on results. Just wait till your baby can do something that your mate's down the road can't. This, of course, all goes out the window when the kid down the road gets into Oxford and your progeny fails their A levels and starts dating a football hooligan skinhead...

Your baby will now sort of parrot and sort of try and say words, usually associated with food. Your baby may even be able to say 'Dad'... Ah! By now you will be almost back to normal at work, as well as a skilled baby carer and have more baby toys, gadgets and furniture in your home than is sensible for any modern couple. If you have swapped cars from a sporty to a baby-friendly motor, then that will also be full of toys, nappies and usually scraps of food.

Is My Baby Measuring Up?

What I found most disconcerting about the many baby books aimed at women (and so-called 'new' men) was the pre-determined timetable of 'success' your baby was supposed to abide by: by such-and-such a stage your baby should be doing x, achieving y, weighing z. I ran a straw poll with all of my interviewees and, bar none, our children, when babies, were in the top percentile for height, weight and cock size during the early weeks. Did this tell us that our children were immensely gifted and superhumanly advanced, or did this tell us that maybe the charts and the algorithms are a little bit out of date...? Well, I for one, initially, liked to believe the former. But with so many peers reporting that their children were also destined for greatness, it became apparent that maybe the model was at fault and that Baby's shape and size (and massive willy) have altered over the last two or three decades, for better or for worse. The fact remains that we are generally bigger adults and, therefore, our offspring follow suit. This is not a bad thing, but it does make a mockery of the so-called progress charts which are supposed to highlight abnormalities from an early age – as far as me and the rest of the dads are concerned, we seem to have fathered the strongest, tallest, most advanced nation of high-achievers the world has ever seen.

Around the time of its first birthday, your baby will start turning into a toddler. They will stand and try to walk and do something called 'cruising', which sounds a bit George Michael, but is in fact just moving from one piece of furniture to another as a way of locomotion. They are often able to propel themselves across the floor like a rocket, so be careful with your cups of tea when strolling about, and don't leave your glass of water on the floor, as your little treasure now has a lot of coordination in all the wrong skill areas – they can grab it before you know it. Hey, those upside-down, topsy-turvy, no-spill cups are the business. More importantly, at this age, whether you appreciate it or not, you baby pretty much knows what is going on too, so if you are going to have an argument with your missus, don't do in front of him. It will scare him.

From 12 to 18 Months – The truth
If you didn't feel particularly close to the young 'un when your baby first arrived, you should be the really proud dad by now. The toddler that has emerged from the baby – surprisingly – is actually fun. They are a bit rubbish at walking, and eating, but it's a whole lot better than it used to be and constantly improving. Hey, you can even

communicate now. They understand what you are saying and can even respond to questions. OK, it is not a full-blown conversation and probably only constitutes a couple of random words strung together, but let's face it, that's not a lot different from the quality of conversation you enjoy with some of your mates. Toddlers are also more independent; you can leave them playing with the Lego or dolls while you have a nice cup of tea and a quick read of the paper, even if you do get interrupted constantly.

The weird thing is that for a while now your little baby has been producing adult turds. Changing nappies is a bit of a chore, to be honest, the novelty has well and truly disappeared... it becomes a lot easier once you can tell your child that you want them to aim for a potty, rather that at random areas of the floor.

All told, I think that one of the best things you can do as a dad is to buy them things they actually like, and to laugh and play with them. If you can also take them with you when you pop out to the shops, willingly as opposed to unwillingly, then you have truly reached the point at which fatherhood is attained.

I Feel Like the Maid Here

And that's because you are. Cooking, cleaning, washing, ironing, scrubbing, waxing, polishing... crap, isn't it? But let's face it, you've been getting away with doing the bare minimum for years. It's only now we truly realize the meaning of drudgery. If ever you catch yourself thinking you've got it hard, just cast your mind back to the all-too-recent images of witnessing the birth, the blood, the screams... and anyway, 'They're your bloody shirts that need ironing,' as my wife kindly reminded me one night when I didn't practise what I preach.

If it hasn't dawned on you already, whatever

household chores you already tackle simply aren't enough. When your baby is tiny you will need to take on not just the lion's share of the tasks, but all of them. Hopefully, this process already began during the pregnancy and you're now a dab hand at cooking, cleaning and tackling the never-ending pit of hell that is laundry. Or maybe it didn't.

The trick to housework is a routine. Just think of it the same way you do your job – certain things get done in a certain order and the quicker you get it finished, the quicker you can get on with your own life. Don't put it all off until Sunday; little and often keeps it manageable.

Cooking
No doubt, if you weren't already a dab hand in the kitchen before the pregnancy, you soon became one. And long may it continue. Cooking can be a ball ache after a day at work, but it's just as appealing after a day of looking after a baby. Use the time to chill out after work and relax – take your frustrations out on an onion and some garlic, and before you know it you've created a delicious and nutritious meal for two, from scratch. You'll be more than happy to receive the kudos. Release your inner Jamie.

Cleaning
There's no dressing up this particular breed of mutton. It's pants, but obviously important, not least because you'll want to keep your home as clean and sterile for the baby as possible. Learn to fit it in – i.e. if you fancy watching something on the telly at 9.00 and you find yourself ready to slump on the sofa at about ten to... stop, get the Hoover out, or the mop; tackle a room and then sit down. One job out of the way, and you're still in time for your programme.

Washing Up
Tackle it straight after eating (in fact, some of it can be

done while you're waiting for the meal to cook). Even though you can't be arsed, it's easier when the sauce left on the plate is still, well, sauce and not a reddish/brown superglue.

Ironing

Don't be tempted to set yourself up in front of the telly – it will take twice as long. Find another room, stick on the radio and off you go. With your partner's clothes check and double-check the correct technique. Women's clothes have an uncanny habit of shrinking and even melting under the care of us blokes armed with well-meaning irons.

Feeling Rather Toasty

Would you regard yourself as a good judge of temperature? I don't mean 'Is this hot or is this cold?' That's easy. But how many times have you been caught out in the cold shivering, even though your partner suggested you wore a coat? Or how many times have you wrapped up warm, only to find sweat beads forming on your brow, in November?

Blokes, in general, have a weird relationship with body temperature. As kids, we would often fight vehemently not to put on a jumper in autumn, or a coat during the harshest winters – our t-shirt was good enough, and, as we all know, coats just make you run slower. As kids we were rubbish at controlling our body temperature; but by virtue of the fact that we ran around all the time, we were OK. Now, that mentality sticks with many of us as we grow older. As the young man about town, despite the rain and the icicles forming over the Yates Wine Lodge front door, we would refuse to wear a coat out because a) it's going to stink of smoke, b) it might get stolen, and/or c) we're too lazy (and tight) to queue and pay for a cloakroom ticket. We might have been cold, but we were man enough to handle it – and that quid we saved on the cloakroom was just enough to get that foxy rock chick at the bar the half-a-snakebite-and-black she wanted... game on.

So, bearing this in mind, we're probably not the best at judging temperature or what constitutes suitable clothing. Now, agreed that men are pretty rubbish at it, well, babies are dreadful. And it's going to be your job to ensure that the house is at its ambient ideal for when your baby comes home for the very first time, and to keep the temperature ticking along at optimum for the next year afterwards. The trick is to buy yourself a cheap thermometer and learn how to work the often intricate, never intuitive, dials of your boiler's thermostat. You should be looking to achieve a temperature of between 18ºC and 21ºC. This is baby nirvana.

Try a Little Resentfulness?

The reality of all those baby clothes drying on the line next to your scraggy boxer shorts and your partner's immense bras should not really be a shock to the system. After all, that's what that whole pregnancy lark was leading up to, wasn't it? We knew that there would now be an extra person living in the house. We knew that babies cry, don't tend to sleep at night-time and place demands on our emotional wellbeing like nothing hitherto encountered. We knew all of this and yet it didn't sink in, not properly anyway. Guess what? You've been pushed down the pecking order and whether you like it or not, you're coming in second to the new arrival. Your partnership with your wife or girlfriend has taken on a new dynamic, essentially a three-in-the-bed scenario (sometimes literally). Up until now your partner has worried about herself and you – that's it. Suddenly, out he pops and your partner has a new favourite... and it's not you.

What's worse, for the insecure among us (and

you're lying if you don't think you're insecure) is that after watching your partner in action with your baby, you get a horrible feeling/realization that they could get on with life, quite comfortably, without you! What exactly is it that you bring to the party? OK, the salary is one thing, but you know instinctively that should your partner need to look after the baby, on her own, from tomorrow, she'd get by – whereas if you had sole responsibility for your baby, would you be able to cope? It's horrible. It's the *fear*. The answer, of course, is yes. You would cope, but you're still going to have those moments of doubt. But that's what makes us great dads – because we actually think enough to worry about such things.

Getting Your Life Back – Will Things Ever Be the Same Again?

First off, don't feel bad. You're not the first dad to suddenly think, *What have I done?* The truth of the matter is, your partner is probably thinking exactly the same thoughts; it's just that neither of you, no matter how close and honest your relationship, feels you can mention your concerns for fear of showing an apparent disinterest or reluctance towards your new role as a parent.

Be cool, here's the low-down on how to wing it... Getting your 'life' back of course depends on what type of person you are and what sort of life you led before you became a dad. If your pre-baby life involved spending your days hanging around shopping centres and street corners, covering train rolling-stock with graffiti, petty theft and drug abuse, then you may not be open to abandoning your 'chav-tastic' playground for the responsibilities of parenthood. But then again, if that were the case, then it's highly unlikely you'd be reading this book. Likewise, if you were enjoying a pre-baby lifestyle as a wealthy, golf-crazy executive bachelor who to your own bewilderment has found himself a dad after succumbing to the lure of Andrea from sales & marketing, then you may just be too dumbstruck to make any reasonable decisions.

But look on the positive side... for the crack-addict, the act of pushing your baby around in a pram gives you somewhere to store your stash. And our executive could hire a dusky East European nanny to help his new wife 'manage', and whom he can, of course, try to *accidentally* catch in the shower. Or, if you just can't handle it at all you can publicly refute you are the father (actually there is a small but shocking percentage chance that this may be true), and refuse to take a DNA test as you are now a Jehovah's Witness. But enough already, for now let's just presume you are an ordinary bloke and be serious...

So we presume you are the dad and are happy about being the dad. You are still in for a bit of a shock. That small humanoid thing that is going to call you 'Dad' has already changed your life, so get used to it. If you believe that 'life', your everyday thoughts and actions, will in some way return exactly to normal after a few months, then you are really seriously deluding yourself. Everything you did before your baby was born will have to change. It may not have to change a lot, but it will have to change. This said, being a bloke, you can use your talent for organizing things into simple routines in a logical way. Not only can you get much of your old life back, by which I mean the FUN bits, you can use the baby situation to your advantage and actually enjoy being a dad to the bargain.

Your Pre-Baby Lifestyle
Let's just set out a scene that we can use as a normal pre-baby life: (Cue – soft, happy music...) You are living in a tiny flat/house because it's cool, near town, work and trendy wine bars and there's just enough space for your

music and your stuff. Your girlfriend/partner lives there too and she has her stuff too and you are both really happy, most of the time. Life is all about going to the pub to watch football; having sex; going to the pub to get drunk with your mates; having sex; going to the pub because your girlfriend is shopping and you are bored; taking short-holiday breaks to Barcelona or going skiing. It also includes a lot of wasting money on gadgets and computer games and, because you're 'trying for a baby', having sex, again. Your car is pretty small but nice and people don't look at it and think 'sad twat'. You like playing your computer games with Dave, which annoys the missus, which strangely makes it more 'naughty' and enjoyable. You may like playing rugby, football, squash or tennis or going mountain-biking on Saturday mornings, then spending a lazy afternoon preparing a delicious meal. You like wasting money on CDs, buying clothes that you refuse to try on in the shop, and more gadgets. You both like visiting friends, going for meals, visiting the cinema and of course having sex. OK, there are BAD things too. You have to visit her parents, who hate you. You have to go to work, a job that you hate, and be a wage slave. Your partner can on occasion be a hormonally charged psycho. And so can you. Generally though, everything is just about perfect. Then you decide to have a baby...

Your Post-Baby Lifestyle
If you read *The Bloke's Guide To Pregnancy* you will remember that it made some pretty sensible recommendations (I hope), which, if you didn't follow in the run-up to your baby's birth, you will surely have instigated by now. This included moving to a suitable bigger house. Changing your nice nippy little VW Golf GTi for a big estate car and sorting out your finances and all those credit card bills you ran up on your short-break

spending frenzy. Even, maybe, changing jobs or taking work seriously, if you didn't before. If not, don't worry, it's all covered later here.

If you approach these necessary changes as a terrible loss of your independence and a sign of rapid degeneration into fatty middle age, then you are going to be a right miserable sod and you are not going to enjoy yourself, or life, ever again. *Be positive*. You have entered a new stage of your life: accept it. To be honest, this was going to happen to you anyway. I'm sure you didn't ever want to end up as some sad, 50-year-old loser sitting in the pub on your own in a brown cardigan, with only a microwave chili con carne to greet you when you get home in the evening.

The House
The house you buy is a step up the ladder. It is an investment and it is a home for your family, Mr Hunter-Gatherer. You have probably made a damn good choice in moving and, guess what, with a little bit of DIY and a few strategic moves over the years, you are going to end up with a much bigger, better home with lots of extra space for your stuff. Your missus is bound to see a move in terms of BIG brownie points, especially if you deliver a house that is in keeping with what she and her mates think is 'very nice'. If you get one that has a 'shed' and a 'garage', you also have hidey-holes to occasionally escape the future hordes of children and somewhere you can store large selections of continental lager. Most of your mates will be in the same boat, so will be unlikely to take the piss. Even if they don't, you will undoubtedly have the last laugh when they eventually get to the same point in their lives.

The Car
The car, well, what can I say? You just have to do it, don't

you? The sacrifice is both noble and should be acknowledged. You are probably going to suffer equally humiliating purchases as your family expands. The clunky estate will be traded in for some 'Mum Bus', probably a large purple Zafira (I have one) or Seat MPV. So what! You can still live vicariously via shows like *Top Gear* (maybe you can have your own stash of car mags hidden in the shed – it would be a marked improvement on all those late 90s issues of *Asian Babes* you deny all knowledge of). And when you start getting some cash back in the bank and you are a bit older, you can buy yourself something totally outrageous – probably a Harley-Davidson or a Humvee. So don't take the piss out of those old blokes you see driving around in swanky new soft-top sports cars; they have probably suffered years and years of driving Ford Mondeo estates, filled with their daughter's pony tack in the boot.

The Money

As for finance, I don't have to tell you that children are expensive. It's not just the vast array of equipment they need at first, from baby bottles to car seats; they will impinge on virtually every financial decision you will ever make. You are not going to be able to waste money the way that you did in the good old days. If you come home with 20 new CDs, don't be surprised if you end up being told to take them back to the shop. The first years are the most difficult, not only as you have just changed car and upgraded your home, but your missus will probably be on maternity leave, which means she is earning less money than normal and when she goes back – *if* she goes back – she may be part-time. And if you both decide to work full time, there are nursery or childminder fees which, even with government subsidies, still leave you out of pocket. So it may take time for you to feel that you can buy what you like, when you like. Most often, having children changes the way you feel about money and about saving. It's called being responsible. *(More about money in Chapter 7.)*

The Job

Work: as the song goes, *'I ain't no wage slave and this ain't no slave sale.'* But, unfortunately, you are pretty much a wage slave. Unless you are some 'Trustafarian' and have inherited big money, or happen to find yourself a big corporate bonus every April, or happen to be the bloke who just won £10 million on the Lotto, you have to go to work. And will have to until you retire or until the great proletarian masses rise up to create a socialist heaven (where you will still, most definitely, have to plod off to work, probably for even less reward).

Work is important when you have new kids. You may have regarded your job as a way of earning beer tokens or paying for holidays and treats, but now you have to change your perspective. Mind you, lots of us also grew up with dads for whom work seemed to be the only important thing in their lives, which was a bit naff to be honest. So you want to try and strike a balance.

With a baby at home, you need more cash. There is a temptation just to do overtime, ostensibly to earn more money but also to steer clear of domestic duties. Work is easier as it is something you know. Nappies etc. are things you don't know and there is still a bit of the idea that they are a woman's job in the back of your mind. But overtime is only ever a short-term fix for cash and it is a poor way to deal with your new family. Seeking promotion or changing jobs is a better idea – you're likely to get more money for the same hours and you may even find it more rewarding.

The decision to change jobs may also be a good idea if you work far away from home. Commuting up to the nearest big city may bring in a bigger salary, but the hours away from home and the travelling can be hard. Remember your workload at home is still going to increase and, certainly for the first few months of your new baby's life, you are going to have disrupted sleep. Lots of men choose to relocate nearer to home as a way of spending more time with their family. Even if there is a drop in salary in the short term, there are benefits – you will have far less hassle, spend considerably less time travelling each day, be able to help at home; and the best part is, you get to see your children grow up.

The (So-Called) Holidays
Holidays also change. Whereas in the past you simply planned your holiday around where and when you wanted to go and how much you wanted to spend, the arrival of a baby changes this equation. When your baby grows up things will return, after a fashion, to this approach, but initially you will have to use your holiday to support your partner at home. From now on the type of holiday you choose and when and where you go will be directly influenced by your kids.

Don't expect to do the same things on holiday either. One of my mates still tells the tale of his disastrous two-week mid-summer holiday to Greece with a newborn, which included him having to buy an extortionately priced small air-conditioning unit which he then had to leave behind in the apartment, and job lots of anti-mosquito spray. Certainly holidays, if you are thinking of going away, should be a short distance away. And check that the place is baby-friendly. If your baby has become a toddler, an old farmhouse and close proximity to rivers are not the best idea.

You may also have to use your annual leave to help out. Your baby is going to have to go and have vaccinations, be taken to the midwife, to clinics and to the doctors. If your wife had a Caesarean, then she will need longer recovery time. You may need time for planning a christening or similar ceremony or for registering the baby's name at the Registry Office. Most importantly, birthdays, Easter and Christmas will also become big times, when everybody in the office with kids will want time off. So overall, you will have to think about your annual leave more carefully, and as soon as possible. You will also need to retain goodwill if you need to take a sickie or need leave for an emergency, so be diplomatic and keep the people who need to know informed of the situation.

Organization is Everything: Time/Space/Routine

This is the truth regarding a happy post-baby lifestyle: organization is everything. Your objective is to try and create a happy and stable life for you, your partner and your child. You want to enjoy your time with them and develop your life as a family together, but you also want to have your own social life. To continue to take part in the activities that you consider part of your own independent life that defines you. This isn't selfish, it's normal. In fact, your partner would like her life back too, so you are both singing from the same hymn sheet; it's just a very quiet song... Some blokes just totally disappear from the scene when a new baby arrives. It is like they have moved to a different town (which sometimes they have). Other dads just try and carry on with their life as they did before, which usually doesn't work, as (quite understandably) they are continually broke, knackered and getting lots of grief at home for behaving that way. The *ideal* way to get the best of your life back and fit it around your new commitments is organization. Look at how you live, where you live and think about how you can make your everyday tasks and duties flow as simply and easily as possible.

It is also about how well you can organize other people. From now on, if you want to go down to the pub and watch the match, you will have to know what time the match is on, (and be honest about it – even the most ardent anti-football supporter can work out, quite quickly, that there's no chance the game begins 'about 5.30'). Plan ahead, notify your wife as to when you are going out and build up brownie points to ensure that you are not in the doghouse when you get back at 10.30 in the evening, on a Saturday, steaming drunk, having been out since lunchtime allegedly for a 'quick pint'. So, blokes, get your timetabling head on. Get your negotiation skills honed and prepare to play your cards close to your chest. Warning: if you don't do this, she will; just when you assumed that you would be off down the Coach and Horses to watch the FA Cup Final, as you have since time immemorial, you could find yourself 'doing Mothercare' alongside the other sad-faced dads who didn't plan!

Organizing Your House
Your home consists of a series of boxes with different functions. Living room, kitchen, bathroom, bedrooms. You must prepare them for the baby and for the toddler that will emerge over the next year. You must get organized and prepare them so that you can look after the baby with minimum fuss, bother or sheer panic!

Tidy Up, You Pig!
The messier the place is, the less likely you are able to find the things you need. Make sure you have set places to store the baby food and the feeding equipment. When the baby starts moving on to solids, repeat. Have bowls, spoons, bibs in known places. Buy proper quality equipment, like sturdy cots, a good high chair and a pram that will actually work rather than one that just looks

trendy. Keep large supplies of nappies, wipes and nappy sacks stored strategically around the house.

How Clean Is Your House?
For many men, personal hygiene is something reserved for special occasions. If you are one of the few who shower each day, whether you need to or not, good for you. For the rest of us, the arrival of a new baby is a rude awakening to just how dirty and downright disgusting we really are.

Enter Baby, clean and pure as the driven snow. Even the dirtiest, smelliest, filth-ridden specimen of mankind suddenly feels a bit self-conscious. That's not to say that he might decide to shower a bit more often. Oh no. Instead we find ourselves vigorously washing our hands at every possible opportunity. I think I emptied a dispenser of hand-wash in about five days when Alia was born. I've touched a door – wash. I've touched my face – wash. I've touched my baby – wash.

Without becoming paranoid, be conscious of all the possibilities of passing on bacteria to your little baby. Yes, there's the argument that a little dirt won't hurt them, and that's correct – but it literally refers to dirt, i.e. mud in the garden that may accidentally be swallowed or rubbed in an eye once your baby is toddling. It does NOT mean a nice bout of the E.coli or salmonella that happens to be on your hands from touching raw meat, or whatever else you were doing immediately before touching your child.

Baby-Proof Your House!
Your toddler is going to learn to sit up, then crawl, then cruise, then walk. They will soon climb. They will have the ability to destroy your most precious stuff. They can injure themselves too. (A&E with a toddler is no place to be and if it's on your watch your missus is going to kill you!) You

must inspect your home with the eyes of a young child, (either get down on your knees, or borrow a Man City fan for the afternoon and observe). If it can open, lock it. If it can fall over, fix it up. If it is down low, put it up high; and if it is valuable, put it AWAY!

Rooms! You and your partner will probably spend most of your time with your new arrival in your main living space. It is important that it is comfortable for you and for her. If she is sitting around breastfeeding for hours, then you don't want it to be on a bean-bag. What you have to do is to modify your main room. Try and sort out those points of general danger like windows, doors and electricity points; and remember: TVs and equipment can be heavy and dangerous. You may also want to sort out some future storage, because by the time your baby becomes a toddler, you will have more toys and junk than you will know what to do with, and so you want to get all that crap away somewhere, quickly.

The Kitchen

The kitchen is the place where most domestic accidents happen. You may actually want to put up a gate to keep your baby/toddler out. A kitchen is full of sharp things, hot things and heavy things. Not to mention all the interesting things that a kid may just want to empty all over the floor or try to eat. You can fit cupboard and drawer restrainers. You can try and keep children out of the kitchen, but the simple safety measure is moving things out of their reach. Move your kettle back from the edge of the worktop and be careful of the oven, boiler etc. (especially when your toddler starts to move about, as they have a habit of creeping up behind you).

The Stairs

The stairs – the ultimate risk. The fear is that babies will go from high to low, very quickly. Buy some gates for the top and the bottom. Don't skimp, it's simply not worth it.

The Bedroom

The nursery/bedroom is where they sleep. Make sure it's not just a cot in a back room you have filled with your junk, there for you to fall over at 2am. Make sure the cot is safe and that you have stores of nappies and so on to hand. If the baby sleeps in your room to start with, then make sure that she has a pleasant, accessible space.

The Bathroom

The bathroom is where your toddler can flood your house, play with your razor, flush your wallet down the loo and, of course, drown. 'Nuff said.

The Garden

And don't forget the garden; it has mud, poisonous plants and berries, sharp stuff and probably a huge amount of cat poo dotted all over the place – whether you own one or not.

Learn the Baby Routine

Here's the deal: If you want to have your own time, then you had better learn the baby routine and the skills involved in upholding it. It is really very simple. First you need to learn how to change a nappy really quickly: open nappy – wipes – nappy off – into nappy sack – more wipes – maybe cream – nappy on. If you take responsibility it will be quick, painless and you will get brownie points.

The Cuddling Routine

Then you need to learn how to deal with their fragility. You may not have noticed, but when babies arrive they are very small, rather like emaciated little monkeys, and they make this 'Waah, Waah' noise which doesn't even sound like a baby. The babies you tend to see paraded by proud parents in prams, or on TV to the accolades of 'What a big lad,' or 'What a beautiful Princess,' or 'What a bouncing baby boy,' are many months old. Newborn babies are bloody tiny; let's face it, that's how they manage to come out of your missus' privates, and even then it's a bit of a squeeze. You should know – you watched it all. The point is, you have to be very careful not to drop them or bang them on doors, fridges or the roof of the car. In fact, the first skill you have to learn is to be GENTLE. Up until now, you may have stomped around the house like an enormous ape who's eaten too much sugar; up until now you may have quite happily slammed yourself down on the sofa with all the grace of an exhausted hippo with a doorstep of a cheese and pickle sandwich and a glass of blackcurrant clasped in your vice-like grip, but now you are going to have to be GENTLE. You are also going to have to become, horror of horrors, aware of the fact that something very vulnerable and delicate now lives in your house... who is not *you*. You can accidentally sit on your dog but you *can't* do that with a newborn baby. You are also going to have to learn to be CAREFUL. Lastly, you are going to have to learn to be PATIENT, because babies work at their speed and not yours and they can't help themselves; they are dependent upon you and if you don't mellow out and realize that it takes time to change their nappies, time to get them in their car seats, to feed and to dress them, then you are going to go NUTS. Very quickly.

The Feeding Routine
The feeding routine will change over the months, but the same basic rules apply: speed and efficiency are key. Your partner will probably breastfeed initially, in which case it is all taken care of. But when, or if, it gets to bottles, it's a

case of getting the bottle ready (microwave sterilization bags are a top tip, rather than the steamer or Milton's fluid). And trust me on this – buy a dishwasher if you don't have one already. Not only will babies become a doddle, you'll suddenly become really keen to entertain. Have lots of bottles, teats and milk powder ready. As the baby becomes a toddler and moves to solids, by all means have some emergency jars to hand, but be ready to do some cooking and be able to prepare finger foods. Later on, get those no-spill cups for milk and water. Toddlers can start feeding themselves and so it gets easier!

The Bath-time Routine
Bathing tiny babies is really nerve-racking at first, but you'll learn to love it. Be confident, and get into the routine of preparing beforehand (i.e. test the water!). As your baby becomes a toddler, bath time will actually become a great laugh – for both of you!

The Importance of Routine

Important for Your Child
Your baby needs to learn about routines, not so much so that they can function better (although it will help), but so that *you* can. Which means that your baby will get to enjoy more of your attention at an hour that is generally more socially acceptable than the middle of the night. Newborns don't differentiate between night and day – their world has been dark for nine months. Over time you will begin to coax your baby to sleep when you sleep and to be active during the day.

It takes time to establish a routine. Initially feeds will play a huge role and hungry babies might want to feed as often as every two to three hours, which takes its toll on new parents. But this will settle down and hopefully in a few months your baby will be sleeping through the night and also begin to have a nap in the morning and afternoon at a set time – allowing you to get on with cleaning up the house, preparing the next meal, or catching up on a bit of sleep yourself! Eventually the two or three daytime naps will be replaced with just one and eventually none (although for a good few months they still *need* the sleep, they just won't do it.)

Babies do like a routine and it's only when you go away for a weekend or get caught out at a friend's house, or at the shops, when baby would normally be tucked up in her cot, that you quickly realize how important and necessary that afternoon sleep really is. It might seem obvious to have to say it, but make sure that where the baby sleeps is dark and quiet (blackout curtains/lining are an absolute must). Get used to the timetable and it will soon become second nature.

As well as having a set time to sleep, babies appreciate set meal times. Although you might be happy to miss a meal, or take a late lunch, your baby or toddler will not. Breakfast, lunch and dinner (and even snack times) must be adhered to, because missing one, even by half an hour, throws the whole day into chaos... and there's nothing more challenging than a cranky baby.

Important for Mum and Dad
Routines can become an annoyance. Invariably, whatever time your partner needs to be doing something, it will never, ever fit into when baby is awake/asleep, fed, not crying, raring to go. This can mean going ahead with whatever it is and upsetting the baby... or not doing it at all. The simplest tasks can take weeks, if not months, to complete for this reason alone. In the early days, mums, when breastfeeding, will know exactly what time of day it is and whether Baby's due for a feed, because her boobs

will be aching to release. She's not going to want to be caught out in public with leaky boobs and the whole day (and night) will be dictated by Baby's feeds.

As the months pass everything becomes easier, but without your own routine it is impossible to keep the house clean, or have food in the cupboards, or clean and pressed laundry. It will all build up to the point where it becomes an insurmountable mountain, and that's not good.

So Much for the 'Weekend'

From the very day that we begin school, weekends have a special place in all of our hearts. For two days we can do what we like, assuming we have completed all of our homework on the Friday evening. As we get older and enter the horror of working for a living and (assuming you don't work shifts, in a hospital or in retail) the weekend is the only chance we get to do all of the little things we need to do around the house, as well as shop, sightsee, entertain and relax. Unfortunately, your baby couldn't give a monkey's whether it's Saturday or a Tuesday, and therefore you and your partner are unlikely to enjoy a weekend lie-in, together, for a very long time. But despite this your weekends will become more precious than ever. This is the only real chance that most dads have of seeing their baby in action for long periods of time, so maybe the early mornings aren't such a bad thing. Use your weekends wisely, both in terms of spending quality time but also in preparation for the week ahead. For once the two of you are around to deal with both your baby and the chores, so get them out of the way so that you can maximize the rest of the week. It's a far cry away from lazy Sundays in a beer garden and takeaways in front of the telly... but it will still be fun, if you're organized.

The Brownie-Point Bank

The brownie-point bank is a sure-fire way for blokes to get things back to normal in a social sense. It is a simple system of barter and exchange. But it has some rules. This system has emerged only recently. From the dawn of time blokes did bugger-all about the house, or presumably the cave. We know this as our dads spent all their time at work, did no housework, couldn't cook and didn't really spend a tremendous amount of time with their children. In our lifetime, this 1950s man has been replaced by 21st-century modern man, who now shares the household duties, often cooks and actively wants to take an interest in and be responsible for his children. However, we are still blokes, so we still have to go out to work. (Of course, many of our partners still have to work too, but we'll assume that she's at home full time with the kid for the moment.) Then when a baby arrives, we now have to do lots of extra work at home, which we kind of feel should really be our 'free time' after putting in the hours at the office.

The worst thing is, although we are supposed to adapt really easily to this new lifestyle, for many of us it's very difficult. Deep down, we are still drawn to our inherent Y-chromosome specialist interests: sex, sport, drinking, eating, spending money and showing off. Blokes are exactly the same as they were in the past; OK, so sport may once have meant watching some poor soul being chased round the Colosseum in Rome by a half-starved lion that has been poked with a stick a couple of times up the backside for good measure, but hey, that's history.

Although sometimes we might secretly like to go back to those times of the 1950s when our dinner was on the table when we got home and our wives considered themselves damned lucky just to be married, we also realize it isn't going to happen. Besides, it's much more fun having regular sex with someone who wears a basque and stockings and likes a drink and a laugh, than getting a lukewarm Fray Bentos steak-and-kidney pie from a house-slave who wears a flame-proof nightie. So the brownie-point system has emerged as the way a bloke with children can get out of the house and pursue some of his traditional interests, once in a while, without having his partner waiting at home, rolling pin in hand, for when they get back.

Let me show you how it works:

Example One:

A bloke wants to watch the European Cup Final, but it is scheduled for a mid-week slot. Ideally he wants to have a few drinks, get home late and be excused any baby duties for the rest of the evening. In which case he simply must tell his wife in advance and then make sure he pays with the brownie points he has saved in the bank. He can either have accrued brownie points already by doing lots of little chores – nappies, baths, cooking (DIY also counts) – or he can offer to do chores in exchange. 'I will make the dinner for you before I go out,' 'You can go into town on Saturday on your own if you want to and I will look after the baby.' The exchange will then normally progress with a few caveats, like 'Don't get too drunk – and don't smoke,' which are often ignored by the bloke.

Example Two:

A bloke wants to go away on a stag night. This requires a much larger amount of brownie points. (The special occasion card can be played, but that is something to be reserved for when you go out and get pissed without telling her and then use it retrospectively.) He therefore announces that he intends to do some task that she wants done that is a real pain. 'I am going to re-paint the living room for you this weekend,' whereupon he calls in his brownie-point exchange, 'Oh, do you remember I said about going to go to Mike's next weekend for that do?'

A great way to earn brownie points is to volunteer to do the shopping. If you take the baby it is a bonus situation. Plus, you might occasionally get a really nice-looking lady coming up to you in Tesco's to have a look. Which leads me to another point...

Babe Magnet

There is a bit of an urban myth that carting a young baby around a supermarket suddenly turns you into a babe magnet... it's not true. Sorry. At least that's my experience. It could be argued that I might be unapproachable whether I'm with child or without – who knows? But thankfully I have the testimonies of all the other blokes interviewed to back me up on this – although women won't be throwing themselves down on the ground, as we might expect; approaching dads (read: you) when holding or pushing a newborn makes you a lot less threatening, less scary, more trustworthy and 'nice'.

But meanwhile back in the real world... another way to get points is to get up early to look after the baby, although this can be difficult if you are working or you are a commuter as you may find you turn into a sleep-deprived moron whilst trying to negotiate the Underground. DIY, however, is just a win–win situation. First off, because you get to be covered in paint and/or brandish a power tool, you get left alone and usually brought a cup of tea now and then. Secondly, it feels like real work and it can add value to your new house. Then there are the obvious ones like changing nappies, and cooking is also generally a really popular option. You can make several meals at once, so freeing up time later in the week and best of all, you can open a huge bottle of wine for cooking purposes, and then drink most of it!

This system only works if you have not married a real battle-axe who treats you as her bitch, or if you are not a selfish, narrow-minded beer monster, but you get the picture. A word of warning: the 'We can go and visit your mother' brownie-point option is a high-scorer – but should be avoided except in extreme emergencies.

What I am basically saying is that you can go out and have fun, but the best way actually is just to get back to the things you like doing, slowly, over time. After all, the missus and the baby are your priority. If you used to play Sunday football, you may have to take a little break, but if you discuss this with your team, they will probably make allowances. And actually, with something like this, which is part of your life, the break shouldn't be too long – after all, it's an activity that is a way of keeping fit so most partners won't object; they want you to go and enjoy yourself, just not to then stay out all of Sunday afternoon undoing all that exercise by drinking lots of beer.

She Needs Time Out, Too

Let's face it, women want to get back to enjoying the things that they used to enjoy, pre-baby, just as much as you do. So both of you need to negotiate and plan and make sure that each knows in advance what the other is doing. Arguments between couples about going out or doing things may erupt for good reasons. She might feel she needs more support. She may be worried, too, about being left alone with the baby; she is not deliberately trying to ruin your hobbies. If you take responsibility and learn the same skills as she has, in looking after your new baby, then it will make life easier for both of you. More importantly, you will build up a real rapport with your son or daughter from an early age.

Partners will naturally be more supportive of each other's activities when they are of benefit to the family. If you are doing an evening course that could get you promotion or are learning new skills, then it's unlikely there will be much objection, whereas if you are proposing to go off for a stag do in Amsterdam there most certainly will. The basic rule is, don't take advantage of the wife, just because she is the main carer or has the boobs full of milk.

Ultimately, the best way for you to get your life back to normal is to help her get hers back to normal. If you enable her to start going out and seeing her friends while you're minding the house and family, then you won't actually need any brownie-points rubbish. It will just be a simple partnership. You should also get back to going out together. Often, when a baby is born and you've both been cooped up for the first six months, you can forget that you actually used to enjoy each other's company. Oh, and you may just start getting your leg over again when she is happier and confident in herself again. Life will never be the same, but it can be just as good; and you can't behave like a teenager forever.

It's OK to Feel Resentful and Bored...

The problem with most 'advice' books, I find, is that they insist on painting an incredibly positive image about the subject and often don't actually tackle any negative aspects head-on. This 'rose-tinted' viewpoint can leave the reader feeling cheated and none the wiser (and, on occasion, thinking that they've got it all completely wrong). The whole point of the Bloke's Guide series was to offer an alternative to that 'softly-softly approach' and recognize, if not celebrate, the fact that we're all individuals, each with a whole baggage-train of angst that is impossible to sweep under the carpet. Yes, we're modern dads interested in the upbringing of our children; yes, we're balanced individuals who can look at situations rationally; and most importantly, we know how to act, react and perform in public.

But what none of us is allowed to say, out loud, and especially to our partners, is what's actually going on inside our heads – that on occasions this whole baby lark can be incredibly boring. If you vocalized that, it might be misconstrued as a disinterest in your child, it would question your unconditional love for your child, your status as a man and, quite possibly, even your suitability as a father...

Well, there are times when we get incredibly bored – baby wakes, baby feeds, baby cries, baby sleeps. Repeat. This can go on for weeks. Just like your child, we crave stimulation, challenge and variety. There are times when your baby's antics simply don't offer that excitement any more. These are not bad thoughts; they're just the truth. And, I would wager, it's just what your partner might be feeling on occasion – but it never comes out. Don't worry! You're not suddenly a bad dad, or incompetent or uncaring. We've all been there. I love my kids dearly, but it doesn't stop me cursing that I wasn't able to fly off to Barcelona for a good friend's stag do recently. Do I resent spending the money and time on the children instead? Of course not, but I still missed the stag weekend...

I think dads, in general, wish away time too much. I was guilty of it myself – thinking: can we just bypass the gurgling, cute stage and move straight on to the 'footy in the park', closely followed by the 'first girlfriend chat'. The novelty of the baby stage had completely worn off by the time number two came along. I don't think I was cruel or twisted to feel like this, I just wanted a conversation with my boy, a chance to be mentor and life coach, a chance to feel like a father rather than a poo-cleaner-upper. A chance to interact beyond being handmaiden!

So here's the deal. You will sometimes catch yourself thinking, *If it wasn't for the baby I'd be off doing such and such.* You'll also catch yourself thinking, *Before baby came along me and the missus had a completely different relationship. I yearn for a world that recognizes the art of oral sex...* It's all completely normal. And they are all thoughts that simply disappear into the ether when you look at your baby and suddenly see the utter love and adoration they have for you in their eyes...

Whom Does Baby Love More?

Well, if you haven't guessed already, I'm afraid that it's Mum. Simple as that. You might prove to be an amusing addition to Baby's world, but you're no substitute for the 'real' thing. I've heard that this is slightly different if you're the primary caregiver right from the start, but even when I enjoyed four months of being the full-time carer for both my children (at about the 14-month stage, both times) the precedent was already set... and no matter how cool a day I had orchestrated for my child, no matter how much we'd bonded, the moment Mum walked in the door I was tossed aside like a broken toy, left to clean up the mess from the day's antics and forced to watch as my wife enjoyed the loving attention of my children and heirs. Was I jealous? Oh yes. Green with it. Expect this to continue for at least another five years...

Plus One

Of course on the flip side of all this selfish, confusing self-pity, we are over the moon about the beautiful baby cooing and dribbling in our arms. This baby, this little bundle so perfect in his babygro, can be picked up with just one hand

and yet commands such adoration and devotion you will wonder how it was possible to live without him.

So, what does fatherhood mean to new dads?
Mark: *Everything. It's totally changed my life for the better.*

Paul: *Everything; I cannot really remember what I did before we had Oliver, even though it's only been eight weeks.*

Owen: *Responsibility, respectability, teaching/educating, providing, laughing, supporting.*

Zazz: *Completion.*

Chris: *Apart from being able to buy toys for him that I want, it means having a reason to be a better person.*

Mark: *It's my life. My kids are absolutely everything to me... They're a part of me. It's almost as though there's an invisible, stretchy cord between me and them at all times. They all say that being a parent changes you, but until you're a dad you have no idea, or at least I had no idea. It focused me by showing me what is meaningful in life. It's as though my kids have taught me what life is about. Life was monochrome, and now it's in colour. It was a picture and now it's a movie. It was crap and now it's great...*

Chapter Five

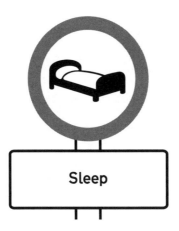

Sleep

As you have probably noticed, babies spend a tremendous amount of time sleeping. In fact, you won't be the first dad to be slightly disappointed that your newborn has hardly batted an eyelid since you first introduced him to his new house (never mind noticed how you must have spent at least four hours cleaning the place). He's fast asleep and you are desperate to get to know him, hold him, kiss him and generally get down to the business of fatherhood! Worry not, this soporific lifestyle is just the calm before the storm. Sleep, or more accurately lack of it, is going to play a very large role in your lives over the coming weeks, months and even years. In fact, the sooner you accept (albeit begrudgingly) that a full night's sleep is a thing of the past, the better.

Baby's schedule is unlikely to be similar to yours (read: the exact opposite), at least not for the first couple of months anyway. While it is true that most babies will sleep absolutely anywhere, you will want to establish the habit of putting Baby to 'bed' when they're tired and that means putting up that cot, if you haven't done so already. Which brings us to your sleeping options...

Found in the Reeds

But way before the cot will ever be utilized, many of us choose to employ the first 'sleep solution' for baby: a Moses basket – a wicker carrier for newborn babies. Some parents prefer the Moses basket to a cot for the early weeks because baby will be a little more enclosed, and after being in a womb for nine months, he is likely to be a bit surprised at all the empty space a cot offers. The Moses basket will keep your baby warm and secure and the handles mean that you or Mum can move him from room to room when you need to – without disturbing the little one. As well as being portable, some Moses baskets come with a stand so that Baby can be raised to bed height, which gives both easy access for you and, more practically, Mum, and also means you can sneak a peek over at your bundle of joy without getting out from under the duvet. The close sides of the Moses basket may help your baby to sleep better in the early weeks.

But all good things must come to an end and your newborn will only be newborn for a very short period of time. Before you feel as if you've even caught your breath after the birth, they're suddenly a few months old and far too long in the body for a Moses basket. Moses baskets are expensive and this limited lifespan is a real disadvantage. Also, starting a baby in a basket and then upgrading to a cot can cause a few sleep problems when you make the switch, as Baby may become unsettled by a change in his sleeping environment. Some parents insist on bypassing the problem by putting Baby in a cot right from day one... the choice is yours and more often than not is dictated by budget or what's available from family members and friends.

It's undeniable that there's something quite cute and traditional about Moses baskets that means many new parents will buy one, or be given or bought one, without really thinking about it. However, although new babies look tiny and vulnerable in a cot, it won't be long until they grow into it.

Whose Crib? My Crib

A crib is something in between a Moses basket and a cot. Just like a basket, it offers Baby a more enclosed environment but its extra length will mean it lasts for about six months instead of about six weeks. Usually made of wood, cribs tend to be very beautiful and seem fitting for your pride and joy.

Most cribs either glide or rock, and this gentle movement can be a great help when you want Baby to sleep but Baby has got other ideas... The raised structure of the crib is useful when you are putting Baby to sleep and retrieving her when she's awake. The fancy looks and the swinging action are all very well, but you're eventually going to have to upgrade to a cot, and just as with the Moses basket, there can a period of disapproval from your baby when you decide to make that switch. Cribs are big and bulky, so you won't be able to cart Baby around the house in one of these; wherever you erect it is where it is going to stay. The big question is, have you got the space?

Whenever we picture a nursery, in the mind's eye, there's usually a crib present – that feeling that they are the norm can be a difficult one to ignore and many a parent has opted for a crib even though they can scant afford it.

Cot-tastic

Cots come in a variety of shapes and sizes and a mind-boggling range of prices. What you are buying is four wooden panels and a mattress – a sleeping area for baby, with a barrier to stop them from falling or climbing out. Cots are good from birth onwards and whatever price you pay, you will get your money's worth.

Cots nowadays are robust, strong and resilient. You may wonder what damage your little angel could possibly inflict on such a large wooden or plastic structure, but it's only a matter of months before Baby turns into Toddler and with that important stage in development comes your child's ability to hit, kick, rage and throw themselves about. When this anger and frustration take place within the confines of a cot you'll realize just why they are so chunky and strong.

Starting Baby sleeping in a cot from birth can be a bit of a shock for them – all that exposed space is daunting and there may well be a few tears and some long, long bedtimes – but you will manage, eventually. Look to buy a cot that has drop-down sides, as this will make it far easier on your bad back, when it comes to picking Baby up out of the cot.

A word of warning: if you do decide to buy a second-hand cot be sure to wash it thoroughly before use and under no circumstances should you use the original mattress – used mattresses have been linked with cot-death. This rule is equally true if the cot was used by one of your own children. Buy a new mattress! When it comes to buying a cot, if you bear in mind that Baby is soon going to grow up and need his own bed, you might consider a cot/bed. As the name suggests, it's a cot until you take the sides off and then it is transformed into a junior bed. A great way to save some cash.

Does This Take Batteries?

Speaking of gadgets, there are occasions, every now and again, that confirm without a shadow of a doubt that men are indeed from Mars... you see, our son, Ronin, quickly became as adept as his dad at sleeping for very long periods of time. But one time he was having an off day; restless, unsettled, whingeing, dead tired, but refusing to go to sleep. We were so unused to this problem that Lisa and I were frantically trying to find a solution. Now, when I heard my wife's request to 'Go and get the vibrating thing,' I thought, *Brilliant, a bit of daytime sex; that will take our mind off Ronin's whimpers of despair...* I ran to our room, disrobed, hopped into bed and waited *eagerly* for an appearance from my wife. She didn't come. And nor, unsurprisingly, did I.

The 'vibrating thing', I found out later, was a reference to the boy's vibrating chair – a colourful sun-lounger rigged up to a battery pack to shake, rattle and roll your baby to sleep. It may sound and look a bit basic, and it is, but this simple device can give whomever has been carrying the little mite for the last hour and a half a welcome break and a chance for their arm and back to recover.

It's simple. New babies like to feel secure, all the time. After nine months of floating in amniotic fluid, the steady beat of a mother's heart, constant warmth and darkness, the outside world can be a harsh and unwelcoming place for the little one. The net effect is that one of you will need to hold your baby constantly. Now, although a vibrating chair won't replace the womb, the gentle movement, comfortable reclining position and safety belt will all make Baby feel that much more secure, buying you or Mum the chance to prepare a meal, go to the loo or just take a short break from being a load-bearing donkey for a few minutes. Babies often go to sleep on the chair. In later months the chair can prove invaluable when you're first starting to spoon-feed. If your child has become used to sitting in the chair, the introduction of solids will be less of a shock than if you are also introducing the wonders of a new high chair. If there are other siblings in the house, strap your baby in and let their brothers and sisters amuse and interact with them. The chair also allows Baby safely to observe what's going on in a room, even if that's just you getting dressed in the morning.

Unfortunately, the vibrating chair does not cut the mustard with every baby. Alia, for whom this device was originally bought, hated it. As with all things, it becomes expensive buying gadgets that your baby doesn't like or use, and there's no real way of testing that until you've bought it and brought it home. Within seconds it will be covered in sick and you're stuck with it. The vibrating chair is all about giving you another option for short periods during the day when you can get on with other things whilst keeping an eye on your little one. If Baby likes it, it's a fantastic investment. If she doesn't, it's just more clutter for your home.

Just Pop 'Em in a Bag

Do you have a wriggler? Sleeping bags for babies are the straightforward solution to keeping your baby warm in her cot. No matter how well you cover your baby with sheets, babies turn and wriggle so much that inevitably the covers end up in a discarded pile in one corner of the cot and Baby wakes up incredibly cold in another. The sleeping-bag option means that they are kept warm by their own body heat all night, no matter how much they move. Sleeping bags are a comparable cost to good-quality blankets and you only really need to have two. I recommend that you buy two exactly the same, so that there aren't any problems in later months when baby learns to prefer one to the other.

Having two identical bags means that you can wash one when necessary and not have to resort to sheets again.

The sleeping bags tend not to offer any protection for Baby's arms, so on cold nights you may have to put a long-sleeve top on your baby so that they don't get chilly. Using a sleeping bag, especially when your child has become mobile, is a great way to prevent any cot escapes. The sleeping bag does make it difficult for Baby to move freely, but the point of putting them in the cot is to get them to sleep, not stretch their legs and jump up and down. Baby can still turn, wriggle and grow and all the time keep snug and warm. Be sure to buy the right thickness of sleeping bag for the seasons she will be using it.

Put the Needle on the Record

Sleep music can be useful for you as well as for Baby. Of course, if you're an overpaid footballer, then a Hoover or a hairdryer might just be the ticket – sometimes we all need a bit of assistance getting to sleep. There's obviously lots of kiddie-specific material available, but nursery rhymes can stimulate rather than relax, and the tried and tested material seems to be more along the lines of either gentle lullabies and instrumentals or New Age stuff featuring a porpoise singing and such like.

We are all affected by the tempos and noises that surround us in life, be they traffic, sirens, chatter from the street or the general noises from within the house, like the humming fridge and the washing machine spin cycle. Babies are attuned to these tempos too, and therefore it is sometimes necessary to encourage a change of pace, especially if it's time for your baby to have a nap. By playing relaxing sleep music you can force a time change and help your son or daughter relax – assuming you've put the correct CD in and the volume is not set to max.

Obviously, if your mates see that whale song CD and the pan pipe albums that have materialized in your collection, then, naturally, they're going to get a bit worried about you. Hide them if you must. The sound of a blue whale mating, or the call of the happy dolphins leading yachts into Melbourne harbour are regarded so highly by so many people that a multi-million pound business has grown, despite many people's scepticism. Don't worry – buying a New Age CD won't lead you down the rocky road of wearing tie-dye clothing and banging bongos of an evening. Not unless you want it to, that is.

Spinney-Roundy-Thing – the Mobile

One of the first decorations or stimulants you will buy for your baby, after his or her first cuddly toy, will be the mobile to hang above the cot. Mobiles can either dangle from the ceiling or else come with a bracket that then can be attached to the cot. A mobile usually has little pieces of plastic, card or fabric dangling from a central frame which gently turns and spins with the movement of air within a room, or by a quiet motor.

There's no denying that if you stick a mobile up above the head of a baby they will stare intently at it and their eyes will follow every movement. I'm sure you could make your own, but that would look a bit tacky really. The cot-mounted mobiles are certainly attractive, thus we buy them, but come the day when baby is standing, or pulling himself up using the cot as support, the mobile will be ripped off and used as a makeshift percussion instrument or a projected missile. The ceiling-mounted mobile will last longer, but when your newborn's eyes are first adjusting and focusing on this strange new world, it could be far too far away to be appreciated.

For very young babies the experts recommend

black-and-white mobiles – babies seem to appreciate the stark contrast much more than looking at primary colours, or worse, pastels. It's up to you to get the stepladder out and get climbing – Baby's room isn't complete until there's something dangling from the ceiling.

Cot-Side Music Box and Light Show
A music box is a common sight in every modern nursery – in fact, if you didn't buy one, you can almost rest assured that a family member did, or certainly intends to! Strap it on (to the cot), wind it up just as you are putting Baby to bed and for a few minutes the box will play a gentle lullaby, helping her get off to sleep. Most music boxes are hand-wound which means the music slowly comes to a stop rather than abruptly switching off – something which might wake her up, just as the snoring had begun. Most music boxes have an in-built light, which sends a projection onto the wall or the ceiling. The volume of the music box is loud enough to be soothing but not enough to startle or scare.

Remember that when your baby gets a bit older and wakes in the morning she will learn to wind the box herself so that the whole house can wake up to the Winnie The Pooh theme tune, but that's kind of cute. It is true that once you have a music box it becomes part of the bedtime routine – reassuring for Baby, especially if she associates it with drifting peacefully off to sleep.

Shadows Playing Tricks

We're not always man enough to admit it, but somewhere in our hazy memory (probably deeply buried, surrounded in concrete and with all maps to the location long since burned) we can recall a time when we were petrified of something really, really scary. For some, it's the quintessential monster in the cupboard; for others, a scary ghost in the garden. For me, for a long while, it was the fear of standing on the lines between paving slabs on pavements. To do so would mean a painful and gruesome death that night (probably involving courgettes and warm milk). It doesn't matter what the rationale – the point is that something can be so horrible and frightening that we are just too terrified to go to sleep without the light on... But we choose to forget all this as parents, and, like our fathers before us, enforce a 'no light zone' at bedtime. But it doesn't work. Light, both in the movies and in real life, represents hope, salvation, comfort, warmth and love – and it makes me think, wouldn't it be a great idea to write and direct a French-language film about the life and times of a humble light bulb, set in a Parisian suburb in 1938, which would inevitably become an instant box-office smash? Or maybe not.

Before long you will realize that your argument about the importance of reducing your carbon footprint and the bid to save electricity curries no favour with your 18-month-old, and that the options available to you are to put on the landing or hall light (thus keeping you and your wife up all night), or find yourself a child-friendly plug-in light.

Basically, this is a low-wattage bulb attached to a plug. You plug it in the socket and from the corner of the room 'shines' a very weak light that often flickers – exciting, romantic-setting effect, or bad circuits? Who knows? Although very young babies don't mind complete darkness, as children begin to get older they do have dreams and nightmares and may start to wonder if the mounted Orc unit currently residing in the cupboard really is waiting to jump out and scare them. Then they start asking for you to leave the door open and the landing light on. The plug-in night-light is the answer. Rather than keeping the whole house lit up, this little beauty emits just enough light to comfort your child without affecting their sleep – or your own. As they get to an age when they start wandering around at night, and especially if they have to pass or use the staircase, the night-light can be strategically placed to avoid any nasty falls. (That counts for you too, you drunkard.)

Prisoner, Cell Block H

There comes a time in every father's life when you have to imprison your own child. Harsh as it sounds and harsh as it is, sometimes it's the only way – hey, we have to be cruel to be kind and all that. Moving Baby from cot to bed is a proud moment for any parent – oh so recently, your child was resident *in utero*, now, suddenly, what feels like a few weeks later, she's bursting out of her cage and ready for the real world – a big bed. But with the removal of bars comes the sudden realization that movement is possible – and that movement is wandering around the house 30 minutes after you've tucked your little gem into bed. Or perhaps quite simply falling out onto the floor.

The solution for the falls is to place a load of blankets, bean bags, spare duvets and teddies on the floor next to the bed, to break the fall. The solution to your toddler's sudden nocturnal wanderlust is a little more complicated. For weeks we tried to reason, but it failed. I'd put our daughter to bed, lie down next to her and we'd say our goodnights (well, I would say goodnight, she'd just grin at me). I would exit the room and go down the stairs. Count five seconds and then there would be the unmistakable sound of footsteps making their way across the landing and the pitiful sight of our daughter standing trapped behind the stair gate at the top of the stairs – in no mood at all for bed. We tried leaving her to moan/wail/cry/scream and occasionally it meant she fell asleep on the landing – which wasn't quite the desired outcome. So then, having caved in, I made the mistake of waiting in her room until she was asleep, but this only became a rod for my own back because then that's what we had to do every night. So, the time came when we decided to invest in a *third* stair gate (bottom of stairs, top of stairs and now across the bedroom door) and employ 'lockdown'. For a while the problems continued, only this time she was crying/falling asleep on the floor of her bedroom instead of at the top of the stairs. Again, not the desired outcome... anyway, in the end, we decided to use scare tactics. Alia liked her door open and the landing light to remain on; our final solution – threaten complete darkness and a shut door. A few 'test runs' to show I meant business and within one evening the going-to-bed-in-a-bed-and-not-on-the-floor problem was solved. Feel free to replicate, and whilst it does feel really cruel, it worked for us and coupled with the 'Stay in your bed for five nights' bribe, we've never looked back. Now it's just the small matter of getting our son to do the same...

In short, I'd say that 'controlled crying', to give it its official term, works when they're very young, but when they're older I think you just need to try to ensure that they're tired out by the activity in the day... then they'll sleep better.

A Brief Introduction to Sunrise...

I love sunrise; I love it so much, I made a concerted and expensive effort to fly halfway across the world, along with a mate, so that we could watch the sun rise on Mount Everest on 1st January 2000. (A pre-child whim!) How smug we felt, as our chums were planning a night of debauchery at the local Yates Wine Lodge and we negotiated to hire a Sherpa, in the backstreets of Kathmandu, to take us up the world's highest mountain – don't get me wrong, we had neither the intention nor the lung capacity to make it to the summit, but Base Camp Everest seemed pretty intense as a significant venue to welcome in the new millennium... Well, Leo, my 'rope partner', and I failed miserably. It transpired that it cost $10,000 for an Everest mountain pass, *each*. K2 was only marginally cheaper... We opted for the third tallest mountain, Annapurna South, which is only slightly shorter than Everest, but, more significantly, free to roam... and for all those pedants reading, Base Camp Annapurna is actually at a higher altitude than Base Camp Everest... so have some of that 'thin air', bitch.

Our millennium trip was a success. (I won't expand too much on the horrors of losing at least six reels of camera film in a hotel room, 'altitude sickness' and a rash between the legs that left me limping my way into the new century – let's just say it hurt a lot, looked terrible and didn't smell too good...) We reached our goal and unleashed a menagerie of cameras to capture the moment. Sweet.

Then along come the kids, or more accurately, Alia, not even a year later. Fast forward a year or two: she's had her eight hours' sleep (if not ten) but unfortunately she went to bed a lot earlier than me... and now I'm the one looking at the clock, willing it to read anything later than 5.45am. Sod the sunrise, I'm tired, and now, back in England, I am willing it to be day. Or more accurately, noon, but that's *never* going to happen.

The Garden Sunrise
In the early weeks, unwilling to exchange pyjamas for mountaineering equipment, most of us opt to wander around scantily clad, our sensibilities disguised with a heavy overcoat, in our own garden or street, pushing a wide-awake child who contrasts with our own dazed stupor. We wander the streets, in slippers, during the pre-dawn, still coming to terms with fatherhood, sex-if-you're-

lucky-and-only-when-you-get-the-chance, and life with a newborn. Once our body understands that this exposure to cold and the associated shivers isn't a brief trip to the outside loo, it does become both enjoyable and rewarding. I promise. There you are – the only non-clubber or milkman awake within 40 miles, pushing your beautiful baby around. For a moment the birds stop singing, the trucks on the nearby dual carriageway pull in, the sound of flushing toilets stops... and it's sunrise. There it is: the purples, the reds, the oranges, the yellows and the strangest formations of clouds, impossible to find in any Collins Gem Guide (I've tried, embarrassingly enough). You, the baby, fresh air, a remarkable future, peace and serenity – and it's not even eight in the morning. What a way to start the day. You get to enjoy it.

What, No Retail?

A few weeks, or months, into this routine and the term 'graveyard shift' takes on a new meaning – it's certainly fun to spend this strange time with the wide-awake youngster, but you're no longer wandering the streets like an inmate on unofficial day-release – no, you're wearing some specialist outdoor walking clobber and are determined to turn the child's walk into a fitness goal, and that's great. But you know the streets a bit too well. You have a 'favourite' place to cross the road and know a certain point 'en route' that ordinarily ends in child-slumber, and in my particular nicotine-addicted state, even a favourite smoking route that ended with a convenient bin for my dog-end. How considerate is that? But it soon becomes evident that it's all becoming a bit of a habit.

It's at this point that we look about for an open shop – a florist, a baker, a candlestick maker – it doesn't matter what. But they just don't exist. A cup of tea and a chat would be hugely welcome, but you're on your own.

Never before have you yearned for company at 7am. The commuters haven't started yet, the radio is still running a late-night 'chill-out' set as opposed to an early-morning 'stick that in your pipe and smoke it' set and you've been up for a couple of hours and are thinking of lunch, even though it's before 9am.

Without doubt the biggest retail growth-industry, should someone have the balls to start it, would be a 'baby shop' dedicated to all things infant – toys, books, accessories and advice, coupled with early opening hours for wandering mums and dads. Each branch could provide a disposable plastic-covered table and promote the café arm of the business. It would work. I'm half tempted to ask the Dragons for some investment... mmm.

Supermarket Sunrise

Your visits to the supermarkets at ungodly hours probably started during your partner's pregnancy. Well, it doesn't stop there. I mean, what did people do before 24-hour shopping? It must have been like living in Tudor England. I know this 'on demand' culture is still a relatively new thing, but how quickly we get used to it. Supermarket sunrise is my favourite – you arrive and it's pitch black, you mount the car seat on the trolley and begin pacing every single aisle only to pick up a Double Decker and a bottle of Oasis. You shimmy past the spilt milk and the mountains of cardboard boxes, pay and exit the store, only to be greeted with the most magnificent explosion of colour. The day has begun. Somewhere between the home-baking aisle and the seasonal goods your little baby re-entered the land of nod whereas you're about to go home and get changed, only to face a gruelling day at the office... but that sunrise has made it all worthwhile (sort of).

Chapter Six

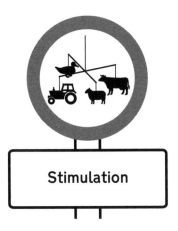

Stimulation

Educate Or Entertain?

If we paid attention to the press, we'd be reprimanding ourselves for simply playing 'pointless' games with our baby. What a wasted opportunity. Why play simple games when every day is a chance to educate our children and begin 'teaching' them in the ways of the world? Well, us dads believe that playing games and interacting, no matter what it is you're doing, is an education. OK, so sticking shapes into the correct holes is not going to help with conjugating Latin verbs or mastering long division (at least not directly) but that's not the point – it's helping with other cognitive skills, and more importantly, it's quality time between Dad and Baby which is an education for both in its own right. To the question, 'Are you trying to educate or entertain?' the responses included:

Mark: *Lots of games. The latest one is I Spy. I am trying to educate as well as entertain, but not in an intense way. I have no plan or timescale for educating him, instead I try to stimulate him and go with whatever he's interested in. For example, at the moment he loves dinosaurs so we went to the Natural History Museum.*

Owen: *Our eldest is bright enough, so we never actively try to teach him anything in stories or play. (We're hoping our youngest will just absorb this intelligence through osmosis.) As for games I guess we do the usual. Hide and seek; we also do stupid dances with music blaring, take it in turns to wear my wife's knickers on our heads while running around the kitchen, paint, we make disturbingly crap models out of clay, fly kites and take trips to the park. If they get to the end of the day and they're not whining, the TV's not been on and they've laughed, then everyone's happy.*

Rhys: *Natasja and I play a game called 'That's my horse'. It comes from a cartoon, Ed, Edd & Eddy, where you dance for a bit, say 'That's my horse' and then inflict some sort of physical impetus on the other person. She usually ends up being thrown across the sofa and I usually end up with sore nads. Most of our games are rough-and-tumbles. The boy is a bit more precious than she was, so has a lower threshold for being scared and thrown about but still enjoys it nonetheless.*

Stephen: *Changes with the years. Entertainment/distraction in the early years morphed into not quite education but intellectual stimulation.*

Zazz: *Both, but mainly to have fun. We like playing games that involve building something, like a train track, or a tower of building bricks that requires a bit of imaginative story telling. Other favourites include picture pairs, jigsaw puzzles, Play-Doh, any card-based games and games that require Daddy to be some form of load-carrying beast.*

Being a dad, for me, is a passport to do all the cool stuff again. In our busy, nine-to-five (if you're lucky) lifestyles, when, oh when, would you ever have the opportunity to visit the aquarium or the art gallery or a national park? Suddenly, you're a dad and you can do all this stuff again and your child will love you for it. My kids are of an age now when they've got into camping, in a big way. Out come all of the equipment, the camping food and the torch and away we go, into the wilds – spending the day playing in the woods, looking at bugs, trying to avoid piles of animal poo and genuinely having fun – me included. You might be able to take the lad out of the dad, but the boy inherent within us all is still very much there. Which brings us to...

Indoor 'Fun' Parks

Yes, I've retaliated against a 12-month-old who was bullying my daughter of a similar age. I'm not proud, but I would do it again, mainly because I didn't get caught. Public play areas are a nuisance; nay, a menace. If a facility is designed for under-twos, there will always be a three-year-old showing off; if it's only for under-fives, a six-year-old will inevitably be prancing about – but what can you do? At first I was really quite militant about it and would approach the apparent parents of said miscreant and demand they remove their older child, but after hearing, 'Or what, you tit?' a few too many times (and that was from the mum) I realized it probably wasn't worth going toe-to-toe with someone over the territorial rights to a ball pond, and promptly backed down. Given the particular girth of one particular mum's muscular, tattooed biceps, I felt it was important not to get flattened, by a bird, in front of my offspring.

And still I kept going back – we're all at a loss what to do when it's raining. The poor child's been cooped up all week and you've either been cooped up with them or stuck at work, so this is it. The weekend. A chance to 'go out'. So you do. You know the idea of a 'fun park' itself is sound, the facilities are actually fantastic and the potential experience for your child is amazing. The only problem is, they're public. Which means other snotty, offensive, dirty, ill-mannered, children-from-hell get to play there too. I'm a big fan of municipal facilities for all; the bit I get pissed off about is when another child thinks it's perfectly acceptable to throw plastic balls at my baby's head, or to stamp on her face, or spit, or pinch, or hit, or bite. You get the picture. Just a bit of common bloody decency. I blame the parents, of course. It's just easier to trip over the offending four-year-old than to face doing jail time for inserting a rattle into the eye socket of the parent, repeatedly.

Inspector Gadget

Kids aren't fooled with the toy mobile phone you try to pass off as the real thing. They're far too bright to fall for that. For a start, it makes silly sounds when you press the buttons, in an American accent, and the network-provider logo isn't quite as attractive as Orange or Vodafone. Secondly, you don't seem to freak out in quite the same manner every time it's picked up, which leads to your oh-so-bright child realizing, very quickly, that this is in fact a diversionary tactic that might have worked very well for the last 48 hours, but its time is finished.

They will want your gadgets and eventually you will give them access... just don't be surprised when it all gets broken.

Sharing

Sharing is hard – even for adults. Even for my wife and me. We forget this, but let me present an excerpt from last night's conversation to explain. I asked:

'I'm going to the shop, do you want anything?'
'No. I'm fine.'
'Are you sure?'
'Yes.'
*'So, if I come back with a bag of Maltesers, you're not going
 to want some?'*
'No.'

And then, surprise, surprise, I arrive home with a bag of chocolate treats and the wife robs the vast majority... and I'm gutted. Should have bought two packets, just in case.

For kids, it's not even as clear-cut as 'Well, you had your chance and declined.' It's not black and white at all. It's just a reaction, an instinctive reaction to a particular trigger. For argument's sake, let's say the object is a toy tractor.

Scenario one – a child appears in my peripheral vision who is playing with something that looks fab, *that I've never seen before*. I want it. Now. I don't care (nor register) that someone else is playing with it. I want it. It's mine. *My precious*. Get out of my way. Get. Your. Filthy. Hands. Off. *My*. Tractor.

Scenario two – a child appears in my periphery vision who is playing with something of *mine*. I've been playing with something else, but now I've been reminded of its existence it does indeed look fab. I want it. Now. I don't care (nor register) that someone else is playing with it. I want it. It's mine. *My precious*. Get out of my way. Get. Your. Filthy. Hands. Off. *My*. Tractor.

For kids, the question of ownership is absolute;

despite your liberal *Guardian*-reading ways, you've given birth to a right-wing megalomaniac who can clearly hear everything you're saying about giving the tractor back, or isn't it time you let Jack have a turn, but who is not listening. For a while you might be tempted to buy two of everything, just to avoid the tantrums and the embarrassing scenes, but you'll soon put an end to that idea when you notice your little one scoop up *both* tractors and still refuse to share. It's a phase, it will pass. It just seems like it takes ages. Our six-year-old occasionally reverts to her über-fascist possessive point of view, usually over something really banal like one particular balloon, even though there are another ten to choose from. And I've already hinted that I revert to my toddler-possessive ways when there's a bag of Maltesers at stake...

Choosing Their Friends

So, there are 14 kids in the playgroup, or the nursery, or at the party, or in the street, or sitting in your lounge because of a 'coffee morning' either you or your partner arranged that is now horribly out of control – it doesn't matter where – but what do you say, or do, or think, when your beautiful baby seems to be fascinated with the one bad egg, the weird-looking one, the one baby or toddler that you instinctively know is a bit different...? Do you feel proud that your progeny is not weighed down with the awful burden of prejudice and pre-judgement from which you obviously suffer if any of the above rings true, or do you secretly wish that your child steers well clear of the 'strange one' with the permanent green snot hanging from his or her nose and only plays with the more regular, 'clean'-looking kids?

Parenthood is like an enrolment into fascism. One minute you're a *Guardian*-reading, charity-giving member of the local pub quiz team and then along comes the baby and you've become a fully-fledged Blackshirt: intent on sending Junior to the local grammar school and willing to airlift him or her out of a nasty situation should that horrible-looking 14-month-old armed with a Postman Pat van come a single centimetre closer to your pride and joy. Why? Many of the dads interviewed admitted to worrying that their child would not 'develop' as well, should their little baby's best mate turn out to be the 'weird'-looking one, or the one who throws terrible tantrums, because their children might copy their 'weird' friend.

I was that dad – trying desperately to manipulate whom my children played with. The benefit of hindsight allows me to reveal that your baby will make friends with whomever he chooses, and you're not going to be able to influence that decision (well, I suppose keeping your child housebound would put you back in control, but that's not really a viable option). Babies and toddlers will just get on with life and your meddling is both unnecessary and unwarranted.

Chapter Seven

Money

The main bugbear facing the majority of us new dads is that small, niggling inconvenience called work. Now, the benevolent New Labour government did give us Statutory Paternity Pay, which probably won't keep you in the life you've become accustomed to (in fact it wouldn't keep you in beers for two days at a Spanish resort), but is better than a smack in the gob. This means you are entitled to take up to two weeks' paternity leave, from the day your baby is born up until 56 days after the birth.

I hope you will have considered before the baby is born just how you are going to take your paternity leave. Most dads choose to take the first two weeks for obvious reasons, but this is a double-edged sword. Just as you and your partner are beginning to get into the swing of things and Baby seems a little bit settled, you're back at work. And just when you need cash most, your pay packet is two weeks' down. Although you are supposed to take the two weeks in one block, a good employer will allow you to break it up so that you can work two- and three-day weeks and so spread it out. If you mix this with annual leave you can be around at home a lot for a good couple of months and that will mean you are really getting to grips with your new arrival. An excellent employer will also just pay you your full wages. It is worth asking, but don't hold your breath.

Spending

Whether we were spoilt rotten as kids or felt hard done by will have no bearing on how we individually react to the act (and value) of present giving. It is completely natural to want to provide the best for your children. As fathers we are often, but not always, the breadwinners in the house, and we have the power to make our child's celebrations (whether they be Christmas, birthdays or whatever) that bit extra special... and therein lies the problem. We want to teach them the value of money, and how one should be careful about frivolous sprees at the pub/bookie's/mate's stag do/health-food shop and then there's the buying of presents. Suddenly, all that careful financial planning just flies out the window, because this is my baby we're talking about and I'm going to make it the most extravagant birthday/Christmas/random Saturday in February that I can.

Avoiding Financial Meltdown
Now you are three, every penny is really going to count. Although no one is suggesting that you should become social hermits, or eat beans on toast every day from now until little Frankie leaves home at 18, there is little point moaning about how expensive children are and how difficult it is to know where the money is going to come

from to pay the electricity this month, when you continue to go out with your mates to the pub a couple of times a week. It might only be 'a couple of pints' but 20 quid every session will soon eat away at your spare cash – cash that would be better kept in the 'family' bank account to cover all of the expenses you already know about, and those you are still to learn about. Don't alienate your friends, just suggest a few tins round at the house instead of going out to the pub – you'll *all* save on the ancillary spending as well: the fruit machine, the bar snacks, the pool table, the taxi and the inevitable kebab on the way home...

If your partner is a bit of a fan of shopping, you wouldn't be out of order to suggest that the Jimmy Choo shoe spending sprees should really stop. There should certainly be a spending freeze on home furnishings and trips to Ikea – you're about to unleash a toddler on your worldly possessions, so in a matter of months everything, and I mean *everything*, will be damaged beyond recognition and repair... This is especially the case with consumer electronics. Make do.

Show Me The Money

I'm not sure how ethical it is, but in our dog-eat-dog world I would personally use any tactics available to help the cause. Becoming a parent is seen as a stepping stone, a rite of passage that turns the 'lad', no matter how old he is, into the 'man'. It's up there with marriage in terms of making people consciously or unconsciously treat you differently, and therefore it would be a wise move indeed to keep your boss informed of how life is going with a newborn – you're not looking for congratulations or a pat on the back, well, not in the literal sense, but what you are looking for is recognition of your new role, and some consideration about how difficult it can be to balance work and life. That recognition may come in a change of circumstances at work. A canny boss will realize that a male employee who has recently become a dad is unlikely to be looking for work elsewhere. If your boss likes you, then this will be a welcome relief. However, the canny boss will also realize that (perhaps incorrectly) there is a chance that the added responsibility of fatherhood may be quickly followed by a realization that you need to be maximizing your income, and that's when cogs begin to turn, hopefully to your benefit. A new baby will mean added cost, so you're probably going to be looking for more money, or you'll have to move on. If you're good at your job, then s/he's going to want to keep hold of you. And here s/he is now – knock, knock. 'Can we have a chat about your salary...?'

Wills

Sorry to be so tedious but it is of paramount importance that you and your partner make wills, if you haven't done so already. Organize a will immediately. Wills are reasonably straightforward and not too expensive (certainly in comparison to the potential legal fees that either you or your partner may incur if you have to sort it out after a death).

All a will is really saying is that you want certain items of property or other investments to go to specific people when you die. Just as you control the distribution of your wealth (estate) when you are alive, these are your instructions after your death.

Dying without a will means that the state wins, and it will be a hard battle for your family to win back what should rightfully be theirs, without at least paying a penalty. Contact your solicitors (or find a solicitor in your local area if you don't have one). If you have any more children in the future then be sure to revisit the will to include him or her – assuming you would like your second child to benefit!

Making It Official

And while we're on the subject of boring but essential stuff, it is your legal responsibility as parents to register the birth of your baby within 42 days. If you're married, then either of you can go to register the birth and both sets of details will be included. However, if you're 'living in sin', as we were when Alia was born, then you will both need to attend so that Dad's details can be included on the register (or you can make a statutory declaration on a Form 16, which your 'lover' can bring with her). If you're not able to attend, or you do not complete the declaration in advance, then your details WILL NOT be included on your child's record...

Asking for Cash. And Getting It...

You've spent the last decade proving that you're your own man. You don't need handouts, you don't need sympathy; in fact, that little place you bought to live in three years ago is now worth £60k more than you paid for it... life is good for the new dad... at least on paper. We've never earned so much money, we've never had such access to credit. Combine two salaries and you can pretty much afford the lifestyle you both want. But it's not enough. By the time the nursery fees kick in, and the added grocery bills and constant nappies, wipes, clothes and ancillary products make an appearance, you're in trouble.

Swallow your pride and broach the subject with your respective families. It's not like most grandparents are going to volunteer to give you cash, given that you've spent the last decade or so making a big deal about being independent. They don't want to rain on your parade, embarrass or insult you, but if you bring up the subject...

If you're short of cash, tell them – don't just say you could do with a handout or a bit of extra cash – that's too vague. Try to qualify what it is that's needed or what the money might be going towards – for example, a pram or a pushchair. Maybe you'd like to start some sort of savings account for your child and a large (or small) deposit to get things started would be really great. Grandparents like to know where the money is going and to be reassured that it is actually being spent on the baby and not on the two of you swanning off for European city breaks every month.

Every Little Helps...

The asking for money shouldn't really stop with parents; in fact, you could involve siblings and extended family in the equation by requesting cash upfront instead of lavish presents at birthdays and Christmas. You know that everyone is going to want to buy your child something, but you may not feel you know your uncles and cousins well enough to ask for 'a cash alternative' without it feeling awkward – well, that's what your parents are for. They'll ask on your behalf to avoid any embarrassments. Maybe a couple of uncles, aunties and cousins could club together and suddenly the pushchair and the cot are taken care of. Suddenly this baby lark is looking a bit more manageable and your family can feel they have truly contributed, rather than spending an afternoon in John Lewis buying a present they *think* is suitable. At the end of the day I'm sure you'd much prefer to have no overdraft and a cot and a pushchair than yet another 0–3-month babygro!

The Sting

And if that's got you feeling a bit serious, here's a bit of light relief... I'm not for a moment suggesting that you be dishonest or deceitful in your dealings, because that would be wrong. But I would like to share with you a tale. This is a tale about chance, location, bloke bravado and props...

The 'prop' was a young baby, in a pushchair, wearing a delightful trouser/jumper combo and looking, without a shadow of a doubt, absolutely stunning. Which by association made me look 'trustworthy'. On wheeling my child into the local branch of a bank (one that hadn't been turned into a trendy wine bar) I took my place in the queue, behind the gaggle of old women who'd got there first (well, they didn't need to change a nappy, find some 'distraction' snacks, pack a baby bag, ensure they had the correct change for the bus or car park... nor had they to worry about carrying all of these trappings, plus a baby, who right at this moment would much rather go for a kip than go for an expedition into town, and especially to a boring bank!).

So I join the queue and immediately my baby daughter is a hit. A real beauty. Suddenly the British public has come over all European – wanting to touch and stroke the vision of gorgeousness in the pram. I stand my ground, happy to accept the compliments and comments and quickly realizing that this distraction is helping abate the boring wait that is the British banking queue.

Finally, it's our turn. We approach the window; the purpose of my visit is to pay in a cheque and convert some unwanted US dollars back into the Queen's currency. By now, the cashier is leaning over the counter to soak in my baby as I continue to complete forms and do everything I'm told. The mandate is complete, I sign and the cashier opens the drawer... It's important to reveal I was returning about $200 and was expecting about £120 in return, given the exchange rate and commission at the time. As is standard, the cashier asked how I would like the money. Using the most sarcastic tone I could muster I replied four 50s, four 20s, a ten and a five... and I got it. Just as I'd ordered. Like something from a Derren Brown experiment.

So, How Much Does It Cost to Raise a Child?

The jury's still out on this one. My interviewees submitted an eclectic selection of figures ranging from a tenner (!?) to £100 million. So I guess we're none the wiser. Studies have shown it can be anywhere from £100,000 to £250,000+ to raise a child from 0 to 18 years, but there are so many variables to bear in mind that I think it's just fair to say that kids are expensive and your plans to retire at 40 may have to be put on hold!

There's a real temptation, especially with a first child, to go absolutely mad, and buy everything brand-new, everything designer-brand – a steadfast mentality of *nil satis nisi optimum* – 'nothing but the best'. But there are alternatives. The NCT, for example, offers sales regularly, where good-quality clothing, hardware and other bits are sold off dirt-cheap. Give it a go. It's not a jumble sale; these are parents, just like you, selling on items to raise the next round of funding for their own child. Wash all the stuff twice before using it, if it makes you feel better...

It's hard, but as I recommend in *The Bloke's Guide to Baby Gadgets*, if you can, think twice before any purchase you make on behalf of your child. I'm not saying she's not worth spoiling – all children are – but sometimes excitement can get the better of us dads and before we know it our finances are spiralling out of control, and all we've got to show for it is a fantastic kid's wardrobe which she'll outgrow in about six months' time and, bizarrely, a Scalectrix set and a PS3...

Don't deny yourselves or your child a treat, but do ensure you don't fall into the trap of daily treats. And if that's got you down, then I leave you with Mark's comment:

There's a saying: 'A dad is a man with a picture in his wallet where money used to be.' Kids are a sacrifice, but they're worth it.

And, when asked about the financial plans he'd put into place for his family's future:

Goodness knows. I'm a bloke. The wife does all that shit. She's ever so good at this stuff, you know. Actually, I do have a pension, but I don't know what it's worth or who it's with. And there is a savings account but I've no idea what's in it. Moths probably.

Chapter Eight

Getting Jiggy. Again

Sexual relations with our partner, post-pregnancy, are a big deal for us blokes. It's a big deal especially because we know it's a subject we need to tread carefully around. And therein lies the problem. When something is bothering us, when that something is not really something we want to turn to our mates about, and on this occasion not even our own mums – who else is there, apart from your partner... and she isn't going to want to know how much your balls are aching to unload, given that she's still in shock at giving birth and is enjoying the experience of having 20 stitches in the place that you'd like to become reacquainted with... you're on your own with this one, son. And you know it.

The Aftermath

You were there, just like the rest of us. There's no point in pretending the birth was anything other than horrific. Soldiers come back from war deeply scarred. Dads come back from births twitching and able to look at homosexuality in a completely new light.

But when the smoke finally clears, or more accurately when everything has been cleaned up, you've been booted out of the hospital and you are sitting comfortably at home admiring your new family, at some stage you are going to get the horn. Now, although your mind might be encouraging you to wait a while, there's just no telling him down there and that's where the problem lies, or doesn't, as the case may be.

So there you are with an ache in your pants that just needs to be released. You know that coming home with a selection of wank-mags will not paint you in the right light, nor will late-night sessions in front of Thai porn websites. (You've already been caught once...) So, what can a man do? Well, you can suffer. Just like the rest of us.

The Contraceptive Talk

It made me smirk (I smirk a lot, not sure why, just happy I guess, plus it stops strangers approaching me with banal questions, which is always a good thing) when Lisa was approached, in her hospital bed, not seven hours after 'passing' a nine-pound baby out of her front bottom, by a lady wanting to engage in a conversation about contraception. Armed with a paper bag chock-full of assorted condoms, the impression this lady gave was, 'Should you fancy a quick shag tonight, you might want to use one of these little chaps.' I mean, Christ. She's just given birth. Literally. As a red-blooded male who thinks a lot about sex, even I was shocked into silence at this remarkable experience.

But yes, contraception does have to be borne in

mind over the coming weeks and months and although they say women can't get pregnant when they're breastfeeding, they can and do. Chances are, no matter what the arrangements were before the birth, you'll be dispatched to the chemist to purchase some condoms. Hold your tongue, she won't take too kindly to any comments along the lines of 'sensitivity', 'Can't feel anything'. 'They're uncomfortable' and all that crap – she's just recently given birth and will be feeling enough sensitivity for the both of you!

What Sort of Exercise Is *That?*
After birth, your partner is going to want to feel 'back to normal' in the downstairs department as quickly as possible – despite what you may think, this isn't purely to satisfy your sexual urges but primarily to prevent incontinence and to avoid prolapse of the uterus! The exercises are simple and if your partner has been going to any antenatal classes, she'll know exactly what needs to be done. Basically, pelvic-floor exercises are all about contracting and relaxing the pelvic floor (a cradle of muscles keeping her insides in) to get it back into shape after the birth. These exercises are absolutely essential and (although your driving force will be for selfish reasons) it would be wise to encourage your partner and remind her to make time for her exercises.

Yes, But When Will It All Be 'Back To Normal?'
This is something that crosses most of our minds. It did mine, and I asked my panel of experts for their experience of the matter. In terms of 'when', the answer is simple – it depends. I can't be more specific. Some dads said they were 'back in the saddle', regularly, as quickly as five weeks after the birth (lucky sods), for others it was 18 months, and for one dad, 'I can't remember any more what

normal was'! I can't stress it enough, every relationship is unique. So you, my friend, will probably find you fall somewhere within that rather wide catchment area of two to 52 weeks. Inconclusive, I know. Sorry. Off to the newsagents with you, m'lad.

It *will* get back to normal eventually, but let's just hope that there's a grace period before Baby Number Two is due to make an appearance and you're back to square one again.

Arranging Sex in Advance

It can be the case that you're both just too damn tired to be thinking about sex, or more likely that when one of you is keen (probably you), the other (probably her) is most definitely not. Some of my interviewees mentioned using the calendar in the kitchen as a sex-night planner – yes, it might seem a bit premeditated and a far cry from your pre-baby impulsive sex-fuelled days... but this is fatherhood. Booking, say, next Friday as the night, allows you both to get all the other jobs that need doing out of the way. You can both *try* to catch up on your sleep by enjoying some un-sexy early nights and hopefully, by Friday, assuming Baby sticks to his sleeping routine, it should be game on. But no promises.

Paying for Sex
Well, I suppose there is always taking this at literal value, but that wouldn't endear you or me to our loved ones. Whilst fatherhood shouldn't be just about accruing brownie points, there's no denying the fact that if you are the one responsible for removing all of the barriers to sex – the laundry, the dinner plates, the ironing, the housework, the sore shoulders that could do with a good rub (without you prodding her with your excited member) and all the other

little jobs around the house that need doing – then the likelihood is you are far more likely to be in store for a reward... there's no guarantee, but at least the house will look lovely.

Getting in Quickies

But wait, it's not all doom and gloom. Sex, eventually, will be back on the menu; you just both might have to be a bit more pragmatic about when and how. There just isn't time any more for the aromatherapy bath, the scented candles, the bottle of wine and the *Songs For Lovers XVII* (free with the *Sunday Mail*), reaching track five before you're both fumbling around with each other's clothing... no, it's more likely to be, 'We've got ten minutes before we're off to your mum's for the afternoon, let's get down to it right now.' And, if you're lucky, it might still leave you enough time to have a shave and change your shirt. For the first two years of your baby's life you won't be winning any 'lover of the year' awards. Sorry. Take it when and where you can get it. Standing up in the bathroom became a firm favourite of ours for some reason, to the point where I subconsciously regard brushing my teeth (in the morning) as some sort of precursor to coitus. Weird. But seems to work when you've got two roving kids in a house – mainly because there's a lock and it hasn't struck the children as odd (yet) that Daddy might need help getting out of the bath, or washing his hair, or cutting his fingernails, or any of the other ridiculous excuses we've been pressed to give on exiting the bathroom, together, at eight in the morning. It even worked on some house guests who had stayed the night. I like to believe.

Dealing With Three In A Bed

Don't pretend you haven't thought about the scenario, at least once in your life. It might have been an unconscious 'dream' over which you had no control, but strangely managed to remember the next morning even though, on every other occasion, your recollection of dreams has faded before the milk has been poured onto your cornflakes. Or more likely, it's something that you have spent/still spend many hours contemplating down to the finest detail (I bet you even know the ideal location, the lead protagonists and what you want them both to wear... or is that just me?). Anyway, the three-in-a-bed scenario is something that blokes do wonder about, along with 'turning' a lesbian and running a harem. Do you see a pattern forming here?

We're committed to our partner, the mother of our child and the love of our life; but our minds wander – and let's face it, we don't actually want it to happen, it's just nice to think about; the same way it's nice to 'spend' this Saturday's Lottery jackpot when we learn that it's a rollover worth £5.6 million. Active imaginations; too much caffeine. That's all it is.

The sad truth is, for the vast majority of us (who tell the truth) our first three-in-a-bed experience is not the realization of dreams come true, it's the reality of fatherhood. You, the missus and Baby. Suddenly your king-size double isn't actually that big. Suddenly, despite having the largest body mass in the bed, you're reduced to trying to balance your body on a couple of square inches. Suddenly, night-time has become really, really crap.

Babies find themselves in your bed for a number of reasons (though the fact that your baby can't actually get into your bed without assistance limits those reasons, don't you think?). Too hot, too cold, not sleeping, strange breathing/noises, unsettled, restless, crying, whingeing – maybe your partner just craves a sensible sleeping partner given the racket you make!

Unless you're a smoker, or have been on the ale, or are particularly tired, there's no reason to take yourself off to the sofa; once Baby's asleep it's well worth trying to sneak the little mite back into his cot, so that you can reclaim your fair share of the bed. Sometimes easier said than done, but if you can rouse yourself at 3am, it's worth it, for all concerned.

Actually, getting out of bed to sleep elsewhere should be a last option, because otherwise you run the risk of it becoming acceptable or understandable, or worse... expected!

Her Worries

Her worries about sex can be an intensely private thing. This is not great when you're trying to extract enough information to be able to help. But, thankfully, I was able to speak to enough women to constitute a cross-section, and here are the findings:

So Sore
There's no hiding from the fact that both a vaginal birth and a caesarean section are pretty traumatic events for your partner's fanny and surrounding areas. For a good while after the birth she will be incredibly tender and sore. Chances are there are stitches that need to heal, and it would be insensitive, to say the least, to be demanding sex at this stage.

Too Bloody
Although it's nothing to worry about, there's also a good chance that your partner will experience a heavy discharge

for up to six weeks after the birth. Surprising as it might sound, the last thing she wants at the moment is for you to be adding your own special ingredient to the cocktail of mucus, blood and general gunge being expelled from her body.

Pelvic Floor Not Ready
She may feel that her pelvic floor is simply not ready yet for the exertions of sex – she's been doing all the exercises, but even the slightest bit of wee leakage will worry her and your unwelcome advances are just going to result in rejection – put simply, sex could still be dangerous; her fear might be that after sex, you might withdraw and accidentally remove her uterus...

Through the Eye of a Needle...
She might not have been watching the event unfold from the same season-ticket-holding viewpoint you had of the birth, but she knows damn well how big her baby is and how petite her vagina is... the net result, 'There's no way my fanny will ever be the same again!' This is a serious fear that may have altered the way in which your partner sees and thinks about her own body. Once again, your advances will be rejected. Be considerate, give her time.

Scarred and Flabby
Coupled with any perceived fanny damage are the very real and tangible aftereffects of giving birth and the resulting 'scars of battle'. For mums who experienced a C-section, there will be a physical mark, and for all mums there will be a 'baby belly' for months, if not years, after the birth – think just how big your partner's belly grew to accommodate your baby. The skin was stretched and now the baby's out, the skin needs time to return to normal. She just isn't feeling all that sexy at the moment and no

matter how sincere you are in encouraging her self-esteem back, it's not looking all that bright an outlook for getting your jollies.

She's Ceased to be a Sexual Being

It is not uncommon for women to feel a sense of revulsion about their own postnatal bodies – due to a combination of all of the above. The trauma of the birth, the alterations to her body and the feeling that her body is now a baby-making machine, rather than the temple of pleasure it used to be, can all have profound psychological effects. She may also have a sense of disbelief that you could possibly find her sexy given what you witnessed – and not just the birth, but the aftermath particularly – the bloodied clothes, the disposable pants, the sanitary towels, the breastfeeding, the 'horror' of it all... again, sex (possibly ever again) is the last thing on her mind.

Exhaustion

Blokes, it's fair to say, have short-term memories. We were keen for our partners to rest as much as they could immediately after the birth, and for a few days positively encouraged it. But as the days become weeks we slip back into thinking that everything is back to normal. We forget that for the last nine months your partner's body has been under attack. Her energy has been leeched, her internal organs literally rearranged to accommodate a baby that was continually growing and demanding more resources. To top this all off was the birth... and now your partner, it is fair to say, is knackered. She has not been able to put her needs first for the best part of a year and this is her chance to finally try to recover both physically and emotionally (whilst in the same breath trying to get her head around the demands of motherhood), and right now servicing your John Thomas is as high up the list as cleaning out the fish tank.

Sex is simply not as high up her agenda as it is yours, and that's something that you will have to accept with a stiff... upper lip. Before you get anywhere near her, your partner will need to expel the demons of her shattered self-confidence. This no-holds-barred self-critique, an inner-body Paxman, if you will, needs to take place, on her rules, on her time and there's very little you can or should do to try to influence the outcome. Your sordid little mind can take some comfort, I suppose, that before your appendages see any action your partner may soon embark on a period of 'self-discovery', which you're unlikely to be privy too, but it is nonetheless reassuring.

Your Worries

The birth will have altered the way you view your partner's nether regions. All of that attention from the medical staff in the delivery room, or in the operating theatre, may well have shattered your illusion that your partner's groin is a private area for just the two of you to enjoy. All that poking, prodding and examining, not to mention the birth itself, may leave you wondering if you ever *dare* have sex again... Some of my panel did have concerns about resuming sexual relations including:

It Might Be Painful
This isn't arrogance. Long after the stitches have healed and dissolved we may worry about how much damage we might do to our partner. We certainly don't want to inflict pain, or re-open wounds or do anything that might hamper the healing process. The good news is that there's not a chance in hell you're going to get anywhere near full penetrative sex before your partner is absolutely satisfied that she is completely healed. That said, your return to the fold shouldn't be marked by introducing vigorous new

positions to your bedroom antics; keep it simple, keep it slow and tender, keep it safe.

What's the Damage?

It's crossed her mind, and it's probably crossed yours too – *just* how is it possible to give birth to an eight-pound baby and not be left, well, wider? Will I be able to feel the sides, will I be stimulated, will I be able to cum? The answer is yes, yes, yes. The human body is an intricate machine capable of withstanding a lot of abuse. Sex feels exactly the same, maybe even better! Some fathers even argued that thanks to a strong programme of pelvic-floor exercises, you could find an 'improvement' to the tightness of your partner's vagina.

Can You Satisfy Her?

And for the insecure among us (that's all of us), we might become worried about whether we'll be able to satisfy our partner. Yes you will, you big stud muffin. Just don't be hell-bent on trying to achieve a double orgasm during the early weeks and months. It's down to both of you to rediscover each other, but you've hopefully got a lifetime together to get it right.

So... One Thing Leads to Another

Despite what's going on with Child Number One, you might be keen to expand the population. Good on you. Twice the babies – twice the fun! But how does having more than one child alter you, your partner and your first child? Mark explains:

With our first child we acted like some Orwellian authority. If they're wrong or disobedient you jump on them (sometimes literally). If they say a word incorrectly you stop what they're doing and correct them (unless it's funnier if they just keep saying it the 'wrong' way). A fight with another child could result in a short but well-structured lecture on friendships.

A second child is different. As long as they're not bleeding they don't need help. It's not that you as parents are more relaxed, you're just too tired to make a fuss. This results in first children turning into National Front pro-Nazis, and second children turning into tree-huggin' hippies. Probably.

I remember a dad from work standing there with a smug knowing grin on his face, telling me something a few days before our second child was due to arrive. He said that when you have your first child you think you have no spare time any more. Then when your second arrives you realize that you used to have a ton of spare time, and now you don't. It's so true. I don't believe life would be that different if we had three, but I could be wrong. And I'll never find out. Never, ever.

Chapter Nine

If you thought that your job was 'target-driven', you're in for a shock when you realize how many targets, goals, averages, percentiles and expectations have been placed on your young baby from the word go. Some of those targets will be stipulated by you and your partner, but the vast majority will be those forced on you by relations, friends, the medical profession, and most shockingly, some random old woman in a supermarket...

This all started with the pregnancy: likelihood of this, chances of that, possibility of something else. Your baby's health book will be absolutely full of ominous blank graphs in which will be recorded various data. Height, weight, speed of growth, how magnificent a willy... and it gets worse... Mark responded:

Do I regard myself as a competitive father? I'd love to say 'no,' but 'yes.' I don't mind if my son isn't the brightest in his class as long as he's happy, but everything you read about babies and toddlers gears you towards insecurity. Our two-year-old can mumble about ten words, when according to the NHS he should know 100 words by now. At first it's all about weight and height. Then it's about when they should be crawling. Then walking. Then the number of words they know. Then the number of words they can use in a sentence. There's always a guideline that they should be near and you wonder if you're doing your job right if they're nowhere near it. It's a lot more prevalent with your first child. By the time the second one comes along you're a lot more relaxed about everything, from punishment to what they find and eat by themselves in the garden, while you're sleeping stood up with your head on the worktop after another interrupted, child-filled night.

Stephen reminds us that:

With a first child I think you can be very aware of the developmental stages that everyone (health visitors, family, friends) expects your child to achieve (e.g. crawls by x, walks by y, and so on), and although I tried to be relaxed about it, it's hard not to feel pressure for your child to do what it's supposed to 'on time'. As they get older the pressure stops.

Meanwhile, here are some other developmental milestones you will quickly become acquainted with:

My Baby's First... Night of Inconsolable Crying

This could be Baby's very first night at home with you, or more likely, sometime within the first month of life. What can you do? You've cuddled, patted, spoken gently, rubbed his forehead, his belly, his back, his arms... still the tears, still the anguish, still the pitiful baby-wailing that is set to the perfect decibel level to maximize your attention through a technology similar to Dolby Surround Sound with a speaker cable right into your cerebral cortex. A few hours of this and you and your partner will be at your wits' end – you're tired, emotional and feel absolutely powerless to help. There's nothing worse and if you are still trying very hard to cope with the shock and reality of fatherhood, it's nights like these that leave you teetering on the edge of sanity.

More often than not, there is nothing seriously wrong with your child and by the morning (when he's finally getting a bit of deep sleep and you're trying to get dressed with one eye still shut) it's all forgotten about. No explanation, no side effects (for Baby, but not for you: you'll be knackered for the rest of the week) and no repeat, for a few weeks at least. This is dependency, and this is also the most blatant example of how much your little baby means to you – your love is absolute and unconditional and your entire focus is not on how crap you're feeling, but on how you can make your baby feel better.

My Baby's First... Wee

Babies wee a lot. But bearing in mind that their bladder is about the size of a marble, this shouldn't come as too much of a surprise. There will be evidence of baby wee in his nappy probably while your partner is still in hospital after the birth. Do remember, especially with boys (but occasionally with girls too) that the sudden temperature change when they're having their nappy changed can cause the little lad to take a wee, all over your hands, shirt, and depending on where the location for the change is, your bedding or carpet. And don't think, 'Oh, it's just baby wee,' and leave it to soak, as within a few days it will stink to high heaven unless you start scrubbing. Sorry, mate.

My Baby's First... Poo

There are two stages really – the meconium and the first 'real' poo. It's obviously great to see that the meconium has been passed (although you're lying if you actually want to be the one who has to clean it up). Darkest black with shades of brown, green, yellow and red – gelatinous in consistency, and a bugger to clean off her legs and bottom. The stuff is like glue. If you're interested, I recreated the colour in Photoshop and the HTML code is #2B2219 – not sure of what use this colour could possibly be, but there you go. Meconium will probably make an appearance either on the day of birth or up to two days later. It's the net result of nine months' build-up of dead cells, amniotic fluid (the same stuff that probably had your baby hiccupping in the womb), bile and mucus. As much as it is a half-hour exercise (exorcise?) to clean the stuff up, its appearance is a sure sign that your baby's bowels are in tip-top shape.

But a real poo – a poo consisting of what has been ingested since birth, is a real milestone. It won't look pretty, it won't smell much better, but in that soiled nappy sits evidence of a profound process – the ability to ingest milk, process the energy and nutrients it contains, and pass the waste. That's biology, that is. The dark black colour of the initial poos will be replaced with more delicate shades of brown and green for the next few weeks. Yes, they do smell, but nowhere near as bad as yours; that is, until they move on to solid food.

On the flip side, these poos mark the start of a two-and-a-half-year (-ish) relationship you have just embarked on, involving nappies, wipes and your child's dirty bum. My boy is just reaching the glorious (if slightly hit-and-miss) road to being potty-trained and my relationship with nappies will soon be at end. Whilst I will miss the baby and toddler life stages, I will not miss the nappies. The novelty, by now, has most definitely worn off.

My Boy's First... Hard on

It's difficult to sexualize babies and toddlers and you'll be pleased you've still got until they reach their teenage years before you have to start seriously worrying about their girlfriends, sexual relations and pregnancy possibilities, but your boy already has all the trappings of a young man... and more than likely, when you're changing his nappy over the coming months, you'll witness his erect willy. I'm pretty certain your boy isn't having explicit dreams of carnal pleasure, it's more to do with the sudden change of temperature once the warm soggy nappy has been removed and a bit of fresh air makes an impact on his exposed 'little soldier'.

My Baby's First... Lifting of the Head

Yes, it's a simple feat. For an adult. But for a wobbly newborn it's pretty tricky. Given how much of their total body weight is their head, you imagine it would take a neck ten times the size and strength to support it... But eventually they manage it. Seeing your baby lift her head for the first time brings tears to the eyes. It's remarkable. So much so, you'll remark to others about it for weeks, even if you don't regard yourself as a 'competitive' dad. This is the first sign of the independence bursting to get out of your baby, who will soon become the toddler you'll all too soon be chasing along pavements to stop them from running out on to roads...

My Baby's First... Food

There comes a time in every baby's life when milk just isn't enough. The official line is that this usually happens at six months, but I am yet to speak with a dad (and I've spoken to a fair few) who didn't start weaning their baby before this supposed watershed. Our two children were on to solids (well, mashed-up vegetable slop) by four months; they were ready for it, lapped it up and still continued to breastfeed relentlessly.

For all of us time-poor/cash-rich wage slaves there is a strong desire for an easy life, and don't those crafty retailers know it. A jar of baby food will put you back, give or take, about 6op. Reasonable, you might think, for a meal. But when you twig that the entire contents consist of half a potato and a quarter of a carrot, you begin to think that there might be another option. And there is. Make it yourself. Boil some veg, or cut up some fruit, turn into pulp and you're done. 6op will keep your child going for nearly a week! More importantly, by making your own you can keep complete control over salt and sugar content, which doesn't affect us big strong adults all that much (unless you're piling it in, every day) but can be dangerous for your baby.

A big negative that I found with baby food in jars, especially for babies just getting to grips with solids, is the portion sizes. These are far too big – resulting in you having to throw most of it away, because it doesn't keep once it's heated (and it doesn't keep beyond 24 hours, once the jar seal is broken). Another downside of the jars of food is that your baby might not like it, which means tossing the lot in the bin (and I bet you thought you'd got a right bargain when they advertised ten for the price of eight). Granted, if your baby doesn't like your homemade concoction it will face the same fate, but at least it was cheaper to make!

Most childcare manuals suggest a cunning plan of making slop *en masse* that can be called upon at a later date – namely to make a big batch of butternut squash and carrot (or any other combination of two-plus fruits or vegetables) and then filling an ice cube tray with said mixture. Once frozen, the portions could then be emptied out into a freezer bag, allowing the production of another batch. Then, come dinner time, one, and eventually two, then three vege-cubes can be defrosted and heated ready for consumption. Cunning.

My Baby's First... Tooth

For some lucky parents, you may not notice your child is 'cutting her first tooth', until it has cut, or in plain English, until you see a bright white tooth has suddenly appeared in her mouth. For the rest of us, you'll know that a tooth is coming a good few days before. Expect a red cheek/s, litres of dribbling saliva and a pretty upset little baby. It's not fun, her teeth are literally breaking through the gum to get into the optimum biting position and there's no clever biology, like osmosis, taking place here, it's just sheer force.

All babies are different but most of the dads interviewed used something cold to try to ease the pain – chilled teething rings, partially frozen flannels, teething gel or even humble fingers rubbed over the sore spot really helped. Your baby biting on something will actually speed up the tooth breaking through the gum, which is great. Unfortunately a common by-product is that teething babies lose interest in feeding whilst they're in pain (or worse, start using your partner's nipple as a teething ring – ow!).

Have Calpol or something similar handy in case the teething leads to high temperatures and expect a few broken nights of sleep because the teeth try to sneak out when no one's looking, and that means Baby will wake...

and that means you will wake too.

My Baby's First... Words

My favourite toddler talking story is from one of my mates, who one day was busy putting up some shelves with his straight-laced father when his toddler waltzed into the room and asked, at the top of his voice, 'Where's my f**king ball?' When he told me the story his face contorted with shame and humiliation as he relived the glare of parental disapproval. 'I never swear in front of my son,' he told me. Bollocks. You may not realize it, mate, but your toddler is a little sponge and they repeat everything that they hear.

Another hilarious thing is that your baby will probably say 'Dad-Dad' or something like it, before it will say 'Mum' or 'Mummy,' not because you have done anything to deserve special treatment, but because it is supposedly easier for them to say. Basically, just like walking, babies and toddlers start talking and making words as they develop and you will have to wait till they are ready. They will probably begin to have the odd 'word' or five from about seven or eight months, normally to do with food or drink, or being lifted up or down, but they will also get very good at communicating what they want by other means. There is such a thing as pointing, you know. There is usually a phase when they really babble away too, which is a bit surreal, but who cares.

Anyway, to cut a long story short, by the time they are about 18 months old many toddlers will have lots more words, and they will try to copy what you say. They may also have great fun shouting and screaming for no apparent reason. Your missus will probably be able to decipher just what it is they are trying to say, but it is often a bit slurred and so try and be patient, you big ox, your toddler is trying to communicate with you! Use your brains to work it out. You know it's either 'I want food,' 'I want water' or 'Please change my nappy, my arse is getting sore.' Remember they learn from you, so talk to them as much as possible. Read to them and describe what you are doing and it will help them learn to talk – oh, and you had better start getting used to using 'Flip' instead of 'F**k' or spelling things out, just like the old country-and-western songs you know.

My Baby's First... Crawl

For a while there you might have started to wonder if she'd *ever* move from whatever position you left her in – like an upturned woodlouse, kicking and hitting whatever was in reach, but unable to right herself. Actually, you might have got used to the status quo, and have mastered a routine that means Baby is happy to play on her play mat/baby gym for a 40-minute session every morning, allowing Dad to read the paper or catch up on some emails. Or more likely, begin to attack the disaster area that is the house after your attempt at making breakfast...

Babies, once they start to crawl, are completely different creatures to the ones you were first introduced to all those months ago. They are inquisitive, cunning and tons of fun – especially if you're quite happy to get onto all fours and give them a race every now and again (prepare yourself for some very sore knees!). Crawling offers your baby an incredible amount of freedom, hitherto never experienced, and whilst we revel in their independence and enjoyment, it doesn't take long to realize that crawling babies are also really quick at getting out of sight and into trouble in what seems like a blink of an eye. Be vigilant and take extreme care when opening and closing doors – babies have this strange ability to have a finger or a hand just waiting to be trapped in or scraped by, it seems, every single door in the house.

And then it all seems to come along in a rush – the pushing themselves up onto their elbows, the rolling over, the crawling, and before long the standing and walking... Basically, just as soon as you get used to one particular baby stage, and even begin to start enjoying it, it all changes again and there's a new challenge for Baby, and for Dad.

My Baby's First... Time Standing

It's like witnessing evolution in your own sitting room. There before you, your baby is becoming a toddler. So far four 'legs' have served their purpose, but the time has come to become bipedal. She'll try very hard for a while, and there'll be a few falls, knocks and the occasional helping hand from Dad... but then she'll get it and smile with such achievement and satisfaction it's infectious. This one small feat is a massive leap into the world of independence and will completely alter how your baby/toddler looks at the world and conversely how the world looks at her.

Even if you baby-proofed your house all those months ago, you need to re-visit safety around the house now. Suddenly her head is so much higher off the ground than it was before, and you realize how many coffee-table corners, shelves and various other simple household items are now at her eye level. Your house has become full of new dangers.

My Baby's First... Steps

Not surprisingly, your baby will start to learn to walk when it is old enough and strong enough to do so. Rather like you, when you are trying to get out of bed having been out till two in the morning and having consumed more beer than a small battleship on shore leave, and you first try to lift yourself up on your own. Then you will try and lift yourself up from your big belly. Then you may be able to sit up on your own and finally you may be able to stand up by supporting yourself. This all takes time, but as we know we can then, just about, walk unaided – usually to the bathroom, to stick our head under a tap. (Toddlers don't do this, of course.)

Often, the first sign of competitive parents (more about these later in the chapter) is when they start bragging about how their baby is only eight months old and yet they are now marching up and down like a trooper. But don't believe it till you see it for yourself; most kids at eight months are only just trying to pull themselves up to their feet using your furniture. Supposedly, the average baby starts walking from around nine months. Competitive parents usually have some sort of walking aid like a miniature Dalek base in which their sprog can zoom about. Some have some sort of bouncer, which is supposed to be fun and to build leg strength, and in which your baby will look like a para. Whether or not it helps with leg-strengthening, it can be loads of fun (our daughter loved having a 20-minute bounce every day, our son tried it twice and hated it...). Babies generally only learn how to stand, bend their knees and sit back down again at about ten months. It must be like getting cramp on a long-haul cheap air flight; you may want to stand up for a bit and walk about, but you can't quite manage it.

Some other babies really can't be bothered walking early. Rather than trying to rush into walking they are quite happy scooting about on their backside or just lazing about. They will, however, rouse themselves enough to lift themselves up to grab your boiling-hot cup of tea or to rip the cover off your latest paperback, so be warned. So if your toddler is slow to start walking, don't worry. For most it is a year before they take their first steps, but some take longer. It does not mean that they are slow at developing; it just means they can't be bothered.

Competitive Dad

We try not to be, we really do, but there's something about being a bloke that means we find ourselves in constant competition with the rest of the world, about everything. When we were boys this may have been who got the best mark for a French test, who can run the fastest or, more likely, who's got the best trainers. (Whose mum bought them Nicks instead of Nike thinking they were doing you a favour? Mmmm. Mine did.) As we get older there's the exam results at A level and university (when you're all desperately trying to convince each other on the morning of the exam that you've done absolutely no work whatsoever, no really, too busy shagging birds and pretending to like smoking – you know how it is...). Then we're unleashed into the workplace and it's all about salary, benefits, size of pension, bonus, company car, Blackberry... the list goes on. And so does our constant competitive nature.

Then along came Baby and now we have something else that we can compare, contrast and show off about. And that's where we come unstuck, because we're battling with other competitive dads, and to make matters worse, competitive mums and to make matters even worse, there's a whole heap of emotion tied up in this little gadget. We're all guilty of it to one extent or another, but if you haven't noticed yet, here's a quick guide to the different types of competitive parents:

The Aggressor
No time for games, this is small-willy syndrome on steroids. They'll just put their best cards on the table and hope to bully you into a response. You know the type: flashy suit, overly large watch, odd tic every now and again, shouts a lot. The conversation veers into crayons or finger-painting and he can't wait to tell you of their trip to Bordeaux and little Sophie's mastery of oil paints, still life and perspective.

The Fisher-King
The coy competitor. Usually male, skinny, a bit nervous around people but desperate to impress. He's fishing. He doesn't want to just come out with it, he wants it to be brought up in conversation, naturally, by unnaturally trying to steer the conversation:

'Lovely stairs you have. Not too steep, nice wide steps.'
'Err. Yes.'
'Great for toddlers, you know. They can climb them, test the waters, blah, blah, blah, our Joseph is up and down our stairs like a shot now. We've got rid of the stair gates. Only 14 months. But he was ready.'

The Faux-Complimenter
The cunning ploy here is to be all self-effacing and non-competitive and yet have your entire script worked out in advance... You know the type: usually female, her fella has too much money and she has too much time on her hands to work on these pathetic ruses. Overly friendly, to the point of freakish, far too interested in the smaller details of your home, family and lifestyle and then, as a throwaway comment will observe,

'Oh, I notice your daughter moves with such grace. It must be ballet?'

'Err, no. She's just turned two, still trying to truly master walking, really.'
'Well, you could have fooled me. Lovely stature. My Isobel started ballet at 20 months. Loves it. She has a grading next week.'

Now, this blatant showing off makes me really angry. But what really cheers me up is not giving them the pleasure of replying in the way that I am supposed to, along the lines of how wonderful it must be to be blessed with such a prodigy. And this isn't just petty revenge – it's mainly because I've forgotten what he or she's talking about because it doesn't involve *my* kids. So I usually just wander off without explanation, and the process starts again with someone else.

Stephen Giles writes in *You're the Daddy*:

When you introduce your baby to other people, they will almost certainly come out with 'Oh, he/she's beautiful.' If they're a new parent themselves (and they do tend to gravitate towards you) you should be aware that they're expecting a reciprocal compliment.

Oh, how true this is – and how appallingly bad I was, and remain, at remembering this. The number of times another parent will ask after the health of my children expecting the response, 'Oh, both fine. Yours?' But that's not what they get. Instead, I launch into a detailed discourse about their achievements, size, humour, outlook on life and recently acquired skills. For example (see, this is a case in point – I'm never one to miss the chance to show off about their skills), Alia is getting really confident on her new bike, without stabilizers, and Ronin finds it highly amusing (as do we) to create new and interesting silly walks when in public places. I could go on. No, I really could go on... And that's the problem. I've had six years to fix this, but I can't. After patiently listening to me rattle on *ad nauseum* about my kids, the person asking the question looks on expectantly for the 'And yours?' but it is not coming, it never does. In fact, I've been talking about mine for so long that I'm now late for something so have to make my excuses and leave... More than likely I can't even remember what this person's child is called, or his wife for that matter. I'm really that rubbish.

My Baby's First... Illness

For a small percentage of new dads, illness may strike almost as soon as Baby is born and I can only imagine how heartbreaking that must be. But most of us will have at least a few weeks, if not months, to enjoy our healthy, able-bodied baby. Life treats us pretty well and then, from out of the blue, comes:

Vomiting
Not the usual milk sick that you've become so immune to, you've accidentally worn it to work on your shirt. No, I'm talking about projectile vomiting, the likes of which even William Friedkin, director of *The Exorcist*, would have thought too outrageous to reproduce. How can so much be contained in someone so small? How can it smell so bad and how come, when it happens it's all in slow motion? And still, instead of managing to direct the stream of sick somewhere that can be easily washed down, you end up ensuring every surface (including the ceiling) manages to get a good old coating of baby puke.

When Alia was first really sick (on my watch) aged about 14 months, I remember the two of us stood still for about a minute looking at each other in complete shock. Alia, I'm sure, was desperately trying to work out exactly what had just happened (it's almost more worrying that she didn't burst out crying), and I was just struck rigid with the impossibility of the fact that the contents of her stomach were now covering the entire floor of the kitchen, and the cupboards, and the French windows and my popping-into-the-garden shoes. The worst bit is what do you do next? The girl is standing bolt upright in the single area of floor not covered in puke but I'm going to have to walk through it to get hold of wipes, kitchen roll, towels, a fire hose – anything.

Babies pick up bugs, viruses, nasty bacteria, germs (call them what you will) really easily. What's remarkable is that, generally, they'll be sick a few times and that's it. Fixed. Occasionally, of course, vomiting can come along with:

High Temperature

A real worry for parents; babies don't just get hot, they seem to burn up. Boiling-hot head, hot cheeks, hot back. Invest in a thermometer – there are lots of digital ones on the market that you insert into the ear, which makes a lot of sense when you're dealing with someone so young who might not take too kindly to a stick being inserted in her mouth, or under her arm, or up her bum.

Thankfully, a bit of Calpol solves most high temperatures, but that's not to say you shouldn't be keeping a real eye on the situation. Talk to NHS Direct if you are concerned.

Coughs and Colds

Coughing for most of us is painful, uncomfortable and really annoying. When your baby gets a bad cough it's actually quite frightening. A bad cough actually affects their whole body, makes breathing difficult and, combined with the snot and the phlegm which often accompany it, can be very unpleasant indeed. Be prepared for what can be months and months of runny noses; some kids never seem to shift them, ever. Always seek medical assistance when you become worried, but don't be surprised if the advice is more Calpol. Keep a good stockpile of tissues in the house, and remember to carry some when you're out and about, you know, just like your mum did when you were a lad...

My Baby's First... Birthday Party – as a Guest

Your baby's and their mates' first birthdays often occur within about an eight-week period of each other. If you're still knocking round with the couples whom you met at an NCT or antenatal group – bearing in mind that you were in the same group because your respective partners were all due to drop about the same time – then this makes sense. But what a hit on the bank balance and on eight Saturdays in a row!

The party itself is probably the first time you've seen the dads since the antenatal meetings, and if you didn't bother going along with your partner to them, well, it's probably your first time meeting everyone there.

Within five minutes the party becomes a comparative/competitive sequence of highlights – a sort of 'our first year' from all concerned. The worst bit is, you go in knowing that's what's likely to happen, and yet you can't help but get involved. It's not that you want to play the game but you get goaded and prodded and provoked and it takes all of your power and courage to stop yourself from blurting out: 'I don't care if your precious Barnaby was standing at eight months, playing grade-eight piano by ten months and shagging birds before his first birthday. He's no different than my baby – he can't talk, he can't feed himself and he can't clean his own arse... you silly witch!'

When the red mist clears, however, you'll respond

with, 'Well, they all develop in their own ways,' when your child has been 'beaten' at doing something remarkable. And with something along the lines of, 'Oh, I'm sure s/he'll be doing it in no time' when the tables are turned...

The best bit about first birthday parties is that they're not really geared around the kids at all (enjoy it, it's the one and only time). There's booze, posh oven snacks, more booze and the women tend to feel their motherhood 'technique' is under scrutiny, so tend to dominate the parent–child interaction, leaving you and the other fellas to feel, well, awkward, compare jobs, comment on the weather and shuffle around the room until it's time to go home. Best to go to these things as the only parent – that way, when it all gets a bit shit, you can immerse yourself in putting blocks into a shape sorter and ignore all those other silly big people until it's time to go home.

My Baby's First... Birthday Party – as Star of the Show

You'd think you were preparing for a major military operation. It might even start to feel like your wedding all over again – the food, the bar, the guest list, the facilities. Your parents will probably want to get involved... and hers. Your respective siblings are all travelling in from around the country and the whole event starts to look like a nightmare of organization...

If you've got anything to do with it, or more accurately, any say in the matter, avoid the above scenario at all costs. Never mind inviting all of those people you've never met out of duty, just make sure the house is jam-full of her mates and your mates, with or without children, of all ages. This is a celebration of life. Your child's made it to one and you don't want to be spending the day introducing yourself and justifying your existence – you want to be partying.

Don't be shy about talking about presents before the event – look, everyone who is coming is going to bring a gift, accept that fact. If you don't say anything, you're going to end up with about 40 babygros (aged 9–12 months) which are already way too small. This is your chance to toddler-fy your baby's room, because your baby isn't going to remain a baby for much longer. You're going to need proper child clothes, a bed, bedclothes, outdoor toys, walkers, Scalextrics, the new PlayStation... ask and thou shalt receive.

If you are unfortunate enough to receive a number of visitors to your baby's first birthday whom you have never set eyes on before, at least make sure you enjoy a bit of adult conversation and get lots of thanks for your generosity and company. Be thankful for small mercies, because at this tender age all the parents hang around at birthday parties; in a few years' time they're just going to turn up with their snotty-nosed kids and then leave... as will you, when it's their turn.

The aftermath will be shocking. Inevitably there will be a few babies at this party and although they will have attendants during their stay, be prepared for the total mess that will be left in their wake: lots of milk sick on the sofa, possibly some poo that escaped, a bin absolutely brimming with stinking, fetid nappies, and a monumental amount of crumbs around the entire house. Not just a few sprinklings here and there, but a veritable carpet of masticated rice cakes, bread sticks, rusks, rich tea and bourbons. To make matters worse, you'll have a stonking headache because you've forgotten what it's like to hit the wine during daylight hours and still you have to contend with the small matter of putting a bewildered one-year-old into the bath and to bed.

My Toddler's First... Tantrum

Around the time of the first birthday parties comes the inevitable fall-out. It's the unfortunate by-product of willing and encouraging your child to think and act as an independent human being. Tantrums are completely normal, natural and common. The important thing to remember is that toddlers wear their heart on their sleeve. One minute they're enjoying life to the hilt. Passers-by look down at your child's contented happy demeanour and cannot help but smile... A second later, although nothing has changed as far as you're concerned, you are now having to cope with the screaming, flailing, (surprisingly strong) ball of swinging arms and legs, previously known as your child. It's physically hard work to get them in or out of the house/car seat/pram/neighbour's garden/shop (delete as appropriate), when they are in a rage. It's also emotionally draining and can cause you to feel untold amounts of rage, anger, embarrassment and helplessness yourself.

Once you've accepted that the tantrums will happen, usually when you're in a public place, and more than likely in front of other parents, then that's half of the psychological battle won. It's hard, but you shouldn't feel embarrassed about your child playing up; what, if anything, is being watched by others, is your reaction to the tantrum. Obviously, losing your rag and going toe-to-toe with an 18-month-old who is demanding an ice cream is not going to win you any friends, although that's what you might be considering in the back of your mind... I find (when the red mist clears) that distraction techniques are best. If I'm really at the end of my tether, then I will usually give in and get them the ice cream (or whatever) but only after they've calmed down, completed the exercise (such as getting into the pushchair) and there's been a muttering of 'Sorry' somewhere along the line. If there's a bit more of my patience left in the bank, then I will agree, but only after we've done something Dad needs to do – like buy a paper – to reassert the authority, show cause and effect, and to take the moral high ground over a small child. Which just feels good...

If it's the first tantrum of the day, and I'm stock-piled on sleep, energy and patience, then I take a far more hard-line route. I will give in to the demands only on completion of the task required, or after a certain amount of time has passed (if they're old enough to understand the big hand of the clock moving), or the mess that is the sitting room has been returned to some semblance of normality, or if there is an agreement that this is the one and only treat of the day... not that the last option actually works, but hey, we can only try.

My Toddler's First... Act of Violence

If you throw a ball to a toddler the chances of them catching it (except by lucky fluke) are non-existent. If you encourage a child to throw a small object, say a small toy car, into the large toy box, even from about a foot away, they'll probably miss...

Projectiles

Toddler coordination is pretty poor. Except, that is, when they're in a rage... you see, when your child is angry, suddenly the laws of physics warp and bend around their grubby fist, suddenly your toddler can see into the fourth dimension and bring order to the space/time continuum. Suddenly a remote control is hurtling through the air at breakneck speed only to hit you square on the cheek, or the eyebrow, or the nose... or the groin. How is it possible? The speed? The accuracy? The acute angle? Anyway, it bloody hurts, and it won't be the only time you'll be under fire from your little angel.

Fists and Feet of Fury

You'd think a punch or a kick from a toddler wouldn't hurt, and if you're expecting the blow, usually it doesn't. But as with their ability to throw to Olympic standard, toddlers have this innate mastery of the martial arts – if there's a weak point, a pressure point, an exposed eye, tooth or existing injury to exploit, then they'll find it, with a precision strike that can leave you howling and screaming in acute pain and, on occasion, possibly even in tears.

Don't fight back, but equally, don't go and hide in the cupboard until the missus comes home – explain (no matter the age) that hitting and kicking are naughty and get on with the task at hand. It was for precisely this situation that the 'naughty step' was first invented.

Who's the Biter?

For about 12 months our daughter went to a private nursery. Every once in a while she'd come home with a bright red welt on her body in which you could clearly see evidence of teeth marks. The incident, more often than not, was noted down in her diary/message book and nothing more was said. But for a period of two weeks it seemed to be happening almost daily, and the nursery would even name the offending set of gnashers. So, there I was spitting bloody murder about Paul or Samuel or Thomas but nothing more was done... And then, the marks stopped. Breathe a sigh of relief. And then the comments started about whom Alia had been biting... Suddenly my daughter was the aggressor, the bully, the piranha.

As with many things, it's a phase, and thankfully one that most toddlers get over very quickly. It's alarming to learn your child is being bitten and almost even more so to learn she is the biter. As with most things, it's generally attention-seeking and testing the boundaries – and as with most things, it was quickly fixed with the 'naughty step'. Quite possibly the best invention, by parents, the world has ever seen.

My Toddler's First... Act of Insolence

I suppose that an 'act of insolence' can be any combination of the above examples – the tantrum-throwing stuff and the physical violence. But the one that hurts us more, especially us insecure blokes, is the rejection (albeit temporary) of Daddy... it's like being struck with a sword through the heart. You've had the little one all day, and overall it went very well, but come late afternoon she needed a nap, but didn't get one; net result: a tired little girl. You have a tiff over the building blocks, leaving the crusts on her sandwiches, or whether to watch more *Teletubbies* or *Dora the Explorer* and there's a breakdown in communications, just as Mum arrives home and is welcomed as the returning Saviour of Normality with an abundance of hugs, kisses and even tears of joy and relief. You think that your partner thinks that your toddler thinks that you're a rubbish dad and have struggled to cope the entire day, when in fact things were going perfectly well up until about an hour ago... and then it comes:

'I don't like daddy,' or,
'I don't want daddy to look after me any more,' or
'I hate daddy.'

Rejection. Words cannot even begin to explain... She doesn't mean it. Really. You'll be able to forgive but not necessarily forget.

My Baby's First... Strike for Independence

None of us consciously wants a 'mini-me'; we want our

children to grow up as independent thinkers, able to make up their own minds and comfortable with standing their own ground when it comes to individual beliefs. We truly want this, yet the fact of the matter is, should you be a football fan and your child, in a few years' time, suddenly decides to support your team's arch-rival, it can be a bitter pill to swallow. So, what's the answer? Well, you could try to get them indoctrinated straightaway by buying your child the baby-/toddler-sized strip and ensuring that countless photos are taken 'proving' her interest in the squad from a tender age... or, you can let her make her own mind up – she'll probably hate football, or rugby, or cricket, or whatever your sport is and excel in something completely different. It's OK to be different.

My Child's First... Talk about Death

A bit of a leap, you might think, from toddler tantrums to death, but you'd be surprised... Apparently, through television, children will witness at least 12,000 deaths before the age of 12. The actual number quoted keeps changing (not least because of the ever-increasing glut of channels now available through most cable/satellite/ Freeview TV packages), but you get the picture. And yet there's supposed to be a watershed to protect the young and impressionable. Don't think for a minute that this is naughty young teens hiring 18-certificate films; this is TV, free to view, available on demand 24 hours a day.

To be honest, there really is no such thing as the 'watershed' in terms of kids being exposed to death on TV, be it fictitious or real. In fact, the watershed has become a bit of joke in my opinion – bad language is dangerous, apparently, can't possibly be broadcast before nine. But 42 people blown up by a car bomb – thats acceptable, let's just explain it in 'rational' terms on *Newsround*. What? I've got nothing against showing kids the way the world really works, no matter their age, but I do have a problem when the powers that be have the audacity to say that x is acceptable and y isn't... so where's this all going? Well, you might have imagined, in your mind's eye, that you're going to approach the subject of sex when your child approaches puberty, and imagined *that* chat you're going to need to have about the dangers of drink and drugs maybe a year or two later... but what about death? Death is something most humans seem to be at a loss to explain even to themselves, let alone to each other. I thought it would come up, as a conversation topic, as and when my children became aware of it – you know, in 18 or so years – giving me plenty of time to prepare a watertight, not-too-lame, not-too-terrifying explanation... and then our two-year-old asks what all the stones are for in the graveyard we're walking through. Now, many parents would argue that I should have opted for a little lie, 'Oh, they're just stones people like to write on,' or some such rot.

Apart from keeping Father Christmas alive (and just this evening, with our eldest, tooth fairies), we're incredibly honest with our kids and refuse to tell them any porkies. The net effect is that she asked and I responded... I explained death, as I see it, and I have traumatized our little girl forever more. Did I do the right thing? I don't know. Occasionally, she randomly breaks down into a quivering mess, whimpering, how she doesn't want Daddy or Mummy to die, ever, because she'll be all alone in the world with no one to look after her... and I feel like a complete prick for not making up a story about how the stones were there for people to write on, nothing more, nothing less. Mummy and Daddy are going to live forever and ever and everything is fine... But then, how do you begin to explain the car-bomb victims, the malaria, starvation, hatred, violence, war? Everything, in fact, that she is going to see on TV, or overhear people talking about. Is two years of age too young to learn about life and death? I don't know. But what I do know is that some kids in the world don't even make it to two.

Chapter Ten

The Outside World

You flew the coop a few years ago now; you've grown from boy to man and on to father. Just when you had the world all sussed out, along came Baby... and the outside world is now somehow different. More importantly, how you react and interact have most definitely changed.

Parking Law – the Multi-Storey

Dads. The rule of thumb is this – ignore those easy spaces you see the moment you enter a multi-storey car park. Yes, they're tempting; yes, there is loads of room for a forward or reverse park and it's even well-lit, which probably means your motor is still going to be there when you return. Don't do it. Walk on by. Or, more accurately, drive on by... they offer a false sense of security. What you absolutely must do is simply follow the signs for the exit. Once you've found that hallowed floor, and only then, should you be on the lookout for a space.

You see, as you have already found out, shopping with a baby isn't easy; you'll avoid it if you can, but sometimes there's no option. So the weekend comes around and you have decided to make a trip to the shops *avec la famille* as you've clearly established that the baby's in a good mood – fed, watered, clean bum. Everyone's happy. The drive to the shops will be a pleasure and you're both looking forward to the retail experience that beckons...

But with the best will in the world, something is very likely to go wrong within the first hour of shopping and that's going to mean that your little angel is going to be kicking off about something or other, really soon. You'll have hardly touched the list of things you were hoping to buy, but Baby's in a strop and there's nothing you can do to make this experience any more pleasant, other than to go home. It is at this point that you get to fight with the car-park payment system, as your baby screams blue murder in her pushchair, and the challenge that is inserting a baby into a car seat when they most certainly *do not* want to be in the car seat is leaving you blue in the face – and then, to add insult to injury, you have to drive up a further 14 floors, mostly stuck behind drivers trying to find a parking space themselves, before you can exit the car park and make your way home. Mate, do yourself a favour and have your car waiting as close to the exit barriers as humanly possible. This is the Zen of car parking.

The Supermarket Queue

The British are famed, across the world, for being the only nation that bothers to form an orderly line, ever. We're fantastic at it – from the early years of lining up ready to go back to class after our lunch hour, to the quintessential 'waiting for a bus', and even the often painful 'waiting to be served in a pub'. We just love to stand in line and, for the most part, most people know the rules and stick to them.

Our European cousins think we're mad. The Spanish, for example, will ask who is last in line, '*la ultima?*' therefore appearing on the surface to recognize that there is a first-come, first-served policy in order. That is until they realize that it's young Pablo serving and as they know each other (just), that's enough of an excuse to shout out a request and bugger who else has been waiting longer. The Germans will premeditate the chance that they might require a selection of sausage meat from the deli later that morning and will have therefore left a towel in front of the market stall to indicate their (possible) intentions and expect everyone else to honour this unspoken code. The French will enter the arena late, make a big fuss about a particular type of cheese and proceed to ignore the queue completely, demanding that they are served next. The Italians will be well-dressed and apologetic in their demeanour, but this is, in fact, a tried and tested tactic to bypass the entire queue and get right to the front – leaving onlookers less upset about the realization that they've been jumped and more in awe about how anyone can wear so much red leather and still look so cool...

But my gripe isn't with queue-jumpers, or the Germans. Far from it. In fact, if you've got the balls, go for it – the British are too 'polite' to actually say anything accusatory against you, so if you can handle getting 'evils' from Rosemary (aged 79 from Kent) then you'll get away with it.

No, my problem is with what goes through the minds of people when they are in a queue in a superstore... You've queued up. You've waited patiently for the inch of space to reveal itself on the conveyor belt so that you can begin to unload the United Nations Aid package-sized trolley you've filled for one week's baby consumption and you're a man possessed – balancing a bunch of spring onions on top of cans of baked beans, a cucumber, a tub of hummus and some broccoli – with a grizzly young baby perched in a baby seat. You want this experience over with, as quickly as possible. But, you see, the person in front controls you. They were there first and they 'enjoy' shopping – it's a chance to get out, a chance to chat with the checkout girl, and a chance for them to upset the delicate balance between a successful pain-free shopping experience with said baby and one that turns into a complete and utter nightmare. I'm talking about the 'dawdler', the scatty consumer, the total-idiot shopper who, having stood in a queue for the best part of 20 minutes, has packed his or her bags with such lethargy that you've contemplated giving them a) mouth-to-mouth resuscitation or b) a hand at packing just to make your shopping experience slightly more bearable.

Despite all this time they've had to contemplate the capitalist tendencies of the supermarket chain, despite the fact that they shop here every bloody week, and despite the fact that it is regarded as common knowledge that you have to *pay* for the goods – only then, only at the post-packing stage does it dawn on them that they need to splash some cash. As an infuriated onlooker you are subjected to the search for the purse/wallet, and when this is eventually found, there is the hunt for the exact money. Oh dear, they haven't got enough... so we now enter the esoteric realm of the payment card. It only takes four numbers – FOUR NUMBERS! – to master the black art of chip and pin but can he remember them? Can he bollocks. Three failed attempts to enter fewer digits than a date of birth and the search continues for a chequebook... Finally the shopping is paid for and the customer is prepared to leave, but just to add insult to injury, during the whole payment debacle, the last items of shopping were not in fact bagged but instead had been wallowing in the packing area wondering if they're ever going to be taken to their new home... so a *million* years later he or she is packed and you are now the 'chosen' customer. By this stage your baby is blue with rage, you've already dipped into the Petit Filou, the bread sticks and the bottle of Vodka and you've contemplated smashing a butternut squash over the 'dawdler's' head... Shopping is a killer. Be warned.

Entrusting Others

Dropping off your baby to a childminder, nursery, pre-school or close relative for the first time is possibly one of the most upsetting experiences available to parents. It is not an admission of failure to employ a third party in the upbringing of our kids – for many families it's an absolute necessity. Yes, it might feel wrong. It might feel for a moment that you have in some way failed them. You haven't. If you can afford to have one stay-at-home parent, then that's great. As for me and the missus, at different periods in our lives, and more importantly our children's lives, one or both of us has been at home to provide full-time care. There have been other times, such as right now, while I'm writing this book, when circumstances have meant that our youngest is looked after all day by a childminder and the eldest is picked up from school by the same childminder until we are able to collect both of them at 5.30pm. I don't think this suddenly means that I love my children any less. I am no less of a parent or a father. This is just the only way it can work for us, right now. You do what you have to do, and no one way is any better or worse than another. What we want in life is not always how it pans out.

The Road Is Long

As a parent, leading your child down the scary road to the big house that is the nursery can be a complete trauma (for Dad, not necessarily Baby). How will she cope? Have I failed as a father? Will she be popular? Who's going to win the egg-and-spoon race? We worry too much. Look at the positives – at home all day with you, your baby would soon tire of your sarcasm and obsession for a football team that wins nothing, not to mention your sad devotion to mundane daytime telly. A nursery offers friends of a similar age, a variety of staff, activities, experiences and stimulation – not that you're a wash-out, but surely you can appreciate how green the grass might be on the other side?

As parents we now have access to a spectacular amount of information about potential nurseries. Websites, word of mouth, advertising, and last but not least – the Ofsted report. The final nail in the coffin for struggling establishments, and the greatest accolade there is for outstanding centres of excellence. It's a buyer's market and you have the power to choose from a very wide selection. Read the reports.

Paying to Play

With the pressures on us all to earn more and consume more, and the price of housing beyond the limits of even a sick joke, it's not surprising most families need two incomes just to keep their heads above water. When you have a child or children, unless there is a willing relative to take on the responsibility of childcare, you have no option other than paying someone else to look after your children. This is an emotive subject and not one for which there is a simple answer. As I said above, circumstances have meant that our daughter went to nursery for a spell and our son currently has a childminder. There have also been periods when I've been the primary carer for both of our children and there have been occasions when we've been flying the flag of the nuclear family, with Dad going off to work and Mum staying at home with the kids. When needs must, I guess, is my only response.

Nursery
Nurseries sometimes get a bad rap. They have often been the focus of exposé-type documentaries in which under-trained, under-paid staff come in to work hung-over and fail to give good care to their young charges, thus painting a bad picture of nurseries around the country and, sometimes, of the 'type' of parents who choose to send their children there. These examples of negligence and, on occasion, verbal and physical abuse are horrifying but are most definitely not the norm.

The trick is to research a potential nursery in the same way you would a potential employer/employee/babysitter/school – you are going to be paying a huge portion of your salary out to this organization and in return for these valuable pounds and pennies you have every right to demand excellent service as standard. I would also look for a nursery that offers the children a little bit of greenery, or at worst a patio, on a site that the children can use in the good weather. The best indication of a good nursery is not the glossy brochure, the stage-managed tour or the testimonials printed on the notice board, but word-of-mouth referrals. If you don't know anyone with children at the nursery in question, ask if the manager would give your number to some of the existing parents and see if they'll speak to you about their experiences. You might even make a new friend out of the process.

Childminder
Registered childminders are really good with children. It's

as simple as that. They wouldn't get into the profession, never mind stick with it, unless there was something to the role far more handsome and rewarding than the salary. Because while it might hit your take-home pay hard every month, if you work out what your childminder actually takes home, it's likely to be barely over the national minimum wage...

Again, there are lots of childminders and the more popular ones will be fully booked. So how do you decide which one of the many listed in the phone book or, increasingly, on the net, is right for you? Well, again, personal recommendation ranks highly, and failing that, Ofsted offer reports the same way they do for schools. I think whether or not *you* get on with the childminder should play an important part in the equation, so bear that in mind when you go for initial meetings. As well as checking out the facilities on offer and seeing how well your baby/toddler warms to their soon-to-be primary carer, see how well you get on with them, too. There is an argument that says boys do better in school if they had a childminder rather than a nursery experience pre-school. I'm sure if you looked hard enough, you could also find evidence to 'prove' the opposite. It's really a personal decision. The childminder offers one-to-one (or, at worst, one-to-three) care for your child for the duration they are in their care. With a nursery it will be nearer to one-to-four (dependent on age) and your child's primary carer will alter depending on your baby's age and staff turnover.

Family Members
Of all the third-party care options, having a family member as a carer is usually the least emotionally difficult as well as the cheapest option – it just really depends on the life stages of your relations and their willingness to 'go through the process' all over again.

A number of my interviewees said that relations (usually grandparents) helped out at least one morning a week for the purpose of allowing Mum and or Dad the chance to catch up on other stuff, or do some work. For other dads the commitment from the grandparents was even more – the full nine-to-five care, with extra help thrown in at weekends. They were all *very* happy with the situation and very happy with the effect on their salary.

Obviously a number of factors will come into play as to whether your parents can assist to this level. If they're both still working themselves, then it would be out of the question. Equally they may be too old to cope with the strain of a baby or toddler all day, every day. And, of course, geographic location is going to play a large part in the equation. However, there was one dad who explained his mother-in-law took the train on a Sunday from Devon to Hertfordshire, looked after the baby full-time Monday to Wednesday and went back home on the Wednesday evening. Serious commitment.

Mr Mum

And last but not least there is Dad. Principal carer, house-husband, stay-at-home dad... put any label on it that you want to, it's an option and should definitely be considered when you're deciding what to do beyond your partner's maternity leave. For one thing, your partner may earn more than you, quite possibly a lot more! Don't be proud, if she's keen to work and you have spent the last few years moaning about office politics, boring water-cooler conversations and having a crap boss, then take this opportunity by the horns. Seriously! It's fun. It's also emotionally and physically draining, messy, far longer hours than nine to five, with no holidays, pension plan, chance of a bonus (unless your partner conceives again, you big stud muffin) and absolutely no salary... but other than that, it's great.

I had the pleasure of looking after both of mine for about four months and it wasn't until that pure 24/7 'in the driving seat' experience of parenting that I really fully embraced and appreciated fatherhood. Whilst it was far harder than any job I've ever had before (manual or tertiary), it was conversely the most rewarding.

I suppose the hardest part, for me, was not having my own 'income' and feeling awkward asking for 'pocket money'. But hey, we have had children together, we share a bed, a house, a love for eating venison and watching 24 – all considered, it became easier to see the joint account as a *joint* account and to remove the supposed guilt of spending someone else's money.

Your First Night Away...

Believe it or not, it's going to happen – as dependent as your baby is, you and the missus are going to want or need to be elsewhere, *sin niños*, just the two of you, some time in the next ten years, and that moment may well expose itself far earlier than you first envisioned. You and your partner (assuming you're not both social lepers) are going to be invited to weddings, parties, funerals, get-togethers and parties for ever more... for a while we send our apologies and over-compensate with gifts or sentimental messages on cards, but after a while, we feel obliged (and also really want) to attend.

Accepting the invitation is the easy bit – it's the logistics of how it is going to work that cause the problems. Who can cope with the trials of looking after your baby? What if something goes wrong? How often should you call to check up? Will your incessant phone calls wake the baby? Will your baby remember who you are when you return? It should be such a simple procedure, but it just isn't.

An extreme case study for you: I won two tickets to the BAFTAs, all expenses paid, with a suite at the Grosvenor Hotel and a limo from the house to the hotel, and back again the next day. OK, so the 'limo' turned out to be a local taxi firm and I managed to make it, just, in the back of a dilapidated Toyota something-or-other, but everything else was very tasty. Anyway, the problem: we'd only just moved to Bedford and although we had a circle of friends, there was no one we wanted to ask to babysit at that stage in the relationship, coupled with the fact that we had not left the girl once, thus far. (She was about 14 months at the time, a little bit over-protective in hindsight.) So, we were in Bedford, my lot were in Birkenhead and Lisa's lot were in Southampton – hardly down the road. After careful deliberation, not wanting to pass up the opportunity for a night, on our own, in a hotel at someone else's expense, we came up with the following solution – I went to work as usual and then got the 'limo' to London on my own. Lisa drove to Southampton during the day and left Alia in the capable hands of Grandma and then took the train to London. We had a great night and then we repeated the travel exercise the next day. Long-winded and expensive, but worth it...

My point is that the first night is hard. But you, your partner, your baby and the carer in question will make it through; it's just getting over that psychological and emotional barrier. This is not a bad thing; this is normal. I suppose the thing you've really got to watch out for is enjoying this return to freedom too much and trying to offload your baby at every available opportunity – I think that that would test the patience of even the most adoring friends and family.

We'd Love to Come, But...
OK, so it's morally questionable, but every now and again we don't feel like driving halfway across the country to an event with a small child. One or both of you won't be able to have a drink, you've got to drive all the way home only a few hours after arriving, and invariably there's going to be lots of crying, nappy-change stop-offs, stress, traffic and have you seen the price of a litre of petrol recently? Use your baby as an excuse (you can even cancel on the morning of the event; in fact, that's more realistic).

'Oh, we were so looking forward to it, but he seems to have a temperature and runny poo – we don't want to take any risks.' There's nothing anyone can say; it would be churlish of your hosts to demand a doctor's note and you've just saved yourself a whole heap of problems.

Conversely, your friends with babies may well do this to you...

Is It Really a Holiday?
Well, not in the sense that you were hoping for. I've already touched on this in Chapter 4, but I am afraid all those past experiences of late nights at the bar and lazy mornings in bed are a thing of the past. Holidays simply take on a new meaning when you have kids in tow. The truth of the matter, at least until they are old enough to spend the afternoon by themselves at the pool whilst you're left to make sweet love to your woman all day, is that holidays are there to give you all a break from the daily grind, but not necessarily give you a break.

Exchange the long commute to work and eating cheap takeaway food for long marches to the nearest shop for forgotten nappies and expensive takeaway food. Picture this and you are halfway there already. But that is not to say that holidays with kids are anything but exciting – they're just different. It is changing your mindset *before* you go away that is critical, rather than trying to react once you are away.

Keep it simple – kids aren't going to be impressed with places that are steeped in historic importance. They don't want anything that involves a coach excursion to see some old rocks that were once grand villas. Oh no. They just want sand, water, junk food for lunch and to be allowed to stay up a few hours later. That's it. Book a holiday for the sake of your own sanity, but go into it with both eyes open.

What You Will Need
Entertainment. Entertainment. Entertainment. It's as simple as that. Never mind the glut of books that you hoped to catch up on over the two weeks, it simply isn't going to happen. A tube of glitter, some drawing paper and a fine selection of felt tips, however, will set you in good stead for a fortnight of relative bliss.

The Camp
Sadly, this isn't going to be the spontaneous 'Let's go camping' bright-idea-on-a-Friday-evening scenario, and with a tent and two sleeping bags packed into the back of a VW Beetle, you're off... Far from it. Camping with babies means trying to put as much of your house into the back of your car as is humanly possible. You'll need it all, you think, and you probably will. Camping is fun with little ones but it's also very hard, very tiring, and any 'benefit' you might have thought you'd get from life in the outdoors will probably be compromised by broken sleep, long walks to the toilet block and, despite your precautions, forgetting something fundamentally important, like the stove.

If you're keen campers and have all the gubbins, then go for it. If it's something you'd just like to get into, then wait a few more years, certainly until they're potty-trained. Do yourself a favour until then and enjoy the luxuries of a hotel, a B&B, or a self-catered cottage.

All the Clutter

You will have noticed it within your house and, as trips at weekends become the norm, you will have also found evidence of it in your car. The clutter, the stuff, or as the cynical will observe, 'The tremendous amount of *shit*' you need to cart around and live amongst when you become a parent. It's shocking. You can't turn around in our house without tripping over something brightly coloured and made of plastic. Every cupboard, every wardrobe, every drawer, every nook contains something belonging to our kids. Admittedly, we bought about half of it and the rest is courtesy of friends and family, but it's there, in the way and there's sod-all I can do about it until they're teenagers – when actually I just suspect it will be replaced by clothes, cosmetics, CDs, homework and my kids' friends, who will probably just appear on sofas, on kitchen chairs, and worse, in our bed. They've taken over. No wonder blokes tend to take up gardening in their forties and fifties – they've got no interest at all in the plants and vegetables, it just means they have an excuse to sit in a shed surrounded by their own stuff once in a while. And that hour of not having to remove naked Barbie dolls, or Lego, or dirty kid's underwear from the chair before being able to sit down in your own house, must be bliss. Absolute bloody heaven.

Chapter Eleven

**Grandparents
and Relations**

A New Family Member Arrives!

When your baby turns up it is usually welcomed by
everyone in both your families. After all, it's a new member
of the family and a part of the next generation. But family
relationships can be a dangerous minefield to navigate.
And this can be just as much the case when a baby arrives
on the scene. If you have just put someone's daughter up
the duff without much ado, without being well known to
the family (or without putting a ring on her finger), then
you may well be in a little bit of hot water. Or if, as a
couple, you are very young, or broke, or occasionally still
like to act the immature idiots, then this isn't going to
make the various mums, dads, brothers and sisters very
happy either. But even if you have trodden the well-
established path of long-term relationship followed by

planned-for children, you may still be surprised to find some awkwardness in some quarters. And hey, if one of your or her parents was a bit odd before you had kids, don't expect them to suddenly stop being like that. This said, having a supportive family and especially warm and participating sets of grandparents around is one of the best things that the new parents can hope for. But before we get onto the happy-family bit, let us look at some different tales just for your amusement. And just in case you need to know.

The Problem of Jealousy
A young couple who had been recently married, and hadn't been too careful, discovered that they were going to have a baby. They kept quiet until they had got past the 21-week mark and then joyously announced it to the future grandparents, who were delighted. Unfortunately her sister and husband, who had been married for much longer, had been 'trying for a baby' too, and had not come up lucky. The sister was not only unhappy, but actively hostile and switched from being a close friend to being a total pain in the arse. They were too young and irresponsible to be having kids, she thought, they must have done it just to spite her – just to get the 'first grandchild'. This all stopped when the sister actually did become pregnant a few months later and now everything is happy families again, with it all being swept under the carpet. But it was a very difficult situation for the couple and the grandparents to deal with at the time.

The Unexpected Support
Another story comes from two mates of mine who were unmarried, living in rented accommodation, with temporary jobs when she became pregnant. The bloke was not exactly flavour of the month with her father and so when

they went back to tell her parents the news, they were expecting trouble. Not so. Her father, who was getting on, not only did not mind, but was delighted. He wanted grandchildren and when the baby was a boy he was ecstatic.

Strange Reactions

It is often assumed that the birth of a child can heal old wounds but this is not always the case. We know a couple who have two children now, ten and eight years old, who have never met their paternal grandfather who disapproved of the marriage. There can also be problems between friends. We know that in groups of friends people often get into relationships with people who have gone out with others from the same circle of friends. In one such case, the decision to have a baby by a couple in a new relationship caused a lasting rift between two old female friends. Another way a baby can change things is demonstrated by a mate's father, who was fine during his daughter-in-law's pregnancy, but who went very odd on the arrival of the baby. Something had clicked; he had now moved into a different generation and he found that terribly difficult to accept. In fact, numerous stories of this kind came to light during my research, some very sad indeed. But in the majority of cases I encountered, friends and family welcomed the news.

What can I say about such hostile or strange reactions? Basically, big events in the history of families provoke deep emotions. If a couple is having difficulty trying for a baby when one of their siblings, in what seems like a casual afterthought, falls pregnant straightaway, then this can be heartbreaking. There is also, whether we like it or not, a very strong biological urge. (I once had a close female friend whose boyfriend would not commit, who started informally 'interviewing' male friends and acquaintances for the role of potential father of the child she so desperately wanted. She is now married, Mr Non-Commitment realizing he was for the high-jump otherwise!)

Because of the levels of status and hierarchy in families, and because babies are seen as a step on the life path, a new arrival can provoke sibling rivalry. It can also make people feel old and out of step or, in the case of lost loves, perhaps that they have missed an opportunity forever. Whatever the reasons for problems with family and friends, a couple with a new baby must not let it affect their happiness. The baby is about their future, about the three of them as a new family, and if others have problems with it, well, that is their problem. There is no point getting too wrapped-up in these conflicts. If you do, you could end up ruining what should be a very special time.

Grandparents

Anyone who has raised children without the help and support of grandparents is, frankly, missing out on a hell of a lot. Having two (or more) sets of active grandparents involved with your baby is just about the best thing a young couple can have to support them. This is the time when you really need all the help you can get and grandparents, when they are supportive, can fulfil numerous roles.

Having grandparents on board is not just about emotional support, but this is very, very important. Let's face it: as much as we may moan about how they raised us, they have at least done it before. A new mother may want to confide in and have the support of her mother, for reassurance and for practical support. Many mothers of expectant women end up lodging at their daughter's house (i.e. *your* house) for the week of the birth, maybe longer. Don't turn your nose up, you'll be grateful for the help too. Fathers-in-law up and down the country can be seen launching themselves into DIY projects, readying houses and flats for the baby's arrival. Many mothers-in-law come back to stay when you have to return to work after your short paternity-leave break – for which you should be eternally grateful. Look at any park or playground, shopping centre or school run and you will see grandparents helping out.

I probably shouldn't mention it, but you find in most discussions with couples with young children that when it has come to the crunch, grandparents have also helped out financially. Many of our friends owe the deposit on their new house or car to their parents. Many more have had the debts they incurred being spendthrift DINKYs (Double Income, No Kids, Yuppies) cleared by an older generation who knew money was worth saving for a rainy day, such as children, not for three foreign holidays a year, every new electronic gadget going and a sushi addiction. When one of my close mate's parents visit, they fill his fridge full of food and buy his girl her school clothes. Many grandparents even put money in the bank for the kids' future. In terms of helping out the grandchildren, the grey pound is worth its weight in gold.

It may be hard sometimes for couples to involve grandparents so closely into their lives. Being part of an extended family is not always easy, but it is a compromise worth making. Rifts can be healed and compromises reached. I know for example that a good friend of mine does not get on well with his wife's parents. There have been long-standing problems, but this does not interfere with the relationship between them and their grandchildren. It may not be ideal, but it works and everybody knows that this is best for the children involved.

Having grandparents nearby can be particularly useful at holiday times or while your partner is still on maternity leave. If you are stuck at work it is great to know that your other half is getting some help. What is more, if you need a break, grandparents are babysitters that you can trust and that Baby loves and trusts.

Interfering Olds

However, grandparents aren't all golden oldies... with some there's always something you're not doing right, or at least that's the impression you get. Be it the temperature of the baby, how few or how many clothes she's wearing, the size of her head, the amount of hair, the way you hold your baby, bath her, strap her into the pushchair...

They're only little comments, and we're told they're meant to be helpful, not critical. But they hurt. In fact they can make you red with rage and ready to toss your closest (before Baby came along) family members out into the street without explanation. It's a difficult situation and one that has caused numerous rows for many of the dads interviewed (and me) over the years.

My advice is to accept that it's going to happen, probably when you least expect it. A throwaway comment or observation that you're going to take as a personal slight against your suitability to be a good dad. It's hard. Really hard, but ignore it – at least until they've gone home in a few days' time and you and your partner can spend hours dissecting just what they said, and ranting and raving to your hearts content. And all without causing a massive family fall-out, which won't do you or, more importantly, your baby, any favours.

So what are the likely trigger points?

Weight

Babies are tiny. Even 18-month-olds are tiny, in comparison to adults. I'll be the first to admit that before reaching two years, some babies do look chubby, but that's good, all they need to do is grow a few centimetres and the chub will fill the gaps. Nothing to worry about. Totally normal. And bearing in mind that we spend the first year or so actually worrying that our baby is a bit on the scrawny side, it's a blessed relief to see a bit of podge. It certainly made me feel a bit better that if one of them decided they weren't in the mood for eating much one day that they had something to fall back on. Yes, so the western world is facing an obesity problem, but that's got nothing to do with a bit of extra flesh on your baby. And the absolute last thing you want anyone to say – be it friend, family member or healthcare professional – is that your child is fat.

Looks

Relations and friends can be cruel, albeit unintentionally. Granted, all men like to be reassured about their paternity and comments about him having your nose or ears never really get boring (although our facial expression may say otherwise). But mums like to be reminded too. Your baby has 50 per cent of her genes as well, and all this talk of your Uncle Albert's nose and Granddad's ears will wear very thin very quickly unless someone (i.e. you) reminds all concerned that your baby also has your partner's smile, or eyes, or beautiful looks...

When You Were His Age...

Comparisons between when you were a tot and your little baby are going to come in thick and fast, probably for the next 20-odd years. I find it incredibly difficult to remember what I had for dinner last Wednesday, never mind what stage of development I may or may not have been at, aged eight months. Your parents (and therefore, your child's grandparents) can apparently remember the month (if not the week) that you first did everything – rolled over, sat, drank from a cup, crawled, stood, masturbated... it's all stored 'up there', apparently, and they've decided to bring this *Mastermind*-winning photographic memory back into consciousness right about the time that you are trying to celebrate and support the ability of your first baby. If your pride and joy has managed the art of lifting his head aged ten weeks then you, your brother or one of your cousins managed it at nine weeks – and not only did he lift his head off the floor, he reached up, took a microphone off a stand and delivered, from memory, the poetry of William B. Yeats, followed by a rendition of Louis Armstrong's greatest hits. If your baby was born weighing in at an impressive 8lb 4oz, then you can be sure that Barbara's daughter (Mum's mate's daughter from the bingo) has just given birth to a 12lb dolphin. If your baby has been sleep-trained since seven weeks and sleeps through for eight hours (if only!), then you can be sure that someone's baby, somewhere, has been sleeping for 72 hours at a stretch and only demands a feed once a month...

As a dad this is hard. We don't want to be baby bores; we don't want to bang on about how good, heavy, strong, beautiful, peaceful, fun our babies are, but when we do decide to invite someone into a bit of intimate knowledge about our baby, the last thing we appreciate, or expect, is someone trying to upstage the poor little mite with the superior exploits of a distant relative, who always seems to be able to do everything so much better or faster or smarter... you see, to dads, that's like someone asking them to come out to the car park. You may as well break a beer bottle on the table, present the remnants in a threatening manner and say, 'Well, come on then, d'ya want some?' Dads will react to such a challenge in much the same way. Sure, polite society will decree that killing someone because they think their child is more 'advanced' than yours might be a bit of an overreaction, but when the insult comes, and you're the dad on the receiving end, polite society can come right out into the car park and get the same pasting that this cheeky bastard's gonna get... See how easy it is – one month you've got a standing order being paid out to Médecins Sans Frontières, the next you've swapped it for a subscription to *Guns & Ammo*.

Fatherhood and the Media

I think dads get a bad rap. The media never tire of portraying dads as totally useless, especially when they're left to their own devices. Yes, they can cope, all by themselves, for an hour or two, but any longer than that and there's going to be an incident, probably involving a burnt dinner, a hyperactive child, a flooded kitchen and a serious accident... According to everything from *Casualty* to major Hollywood blockbusters, we're crap...

How did some of my interviewees see themselves portrayed in the media?

Mark: *Very badly. I am a stay-at-home dad, and as far as I can see this role doesn't appear in the media. As for fatherhood in general, I think it's not portrayed well because being a good father is not interesting or funny. Nearly all the fathers I know are very involved, caring and conscientious, but fathers in the media tend to be absent or incompetent or both. You very rarely see a man being portrayed as being competent with his family or in the home.*

Richard: *Fatherhood is only newsworthy or interesting when it goes wrong. Nobody's interested in the safe, secure, mutually enriching situations that predominate. We want to see fathers holding their children by the legs out of seventh-floor windows, apparently.*

Paul: *You only ever hear or see poor examples of*

fatherhood. I suppose I can sympathize with the Fathers for Justice campaigners; I am not especially politically minded, but if their sole aim is to be able to be a positive influence on the child, then they should be supported, not stopped. Mothers are obviously important, but the impact of a father on a child's life, especially at an early stage, should not be underestimated.

It is difficult now, I always think twice about taking pictures of Oliver in the bath etc. as the perception of other people who do not know me from Adam is always going to be negative.

Owen: *Working dads always away. Lots of infidelity. One-parent families always with the mothers.*

Zazz: *We get a bad rap. Men should be put on a par with women at the Family Court. In general, I think that fatherhood is treated as being a fashion statement. Take Beckham for example. Furthermore, I can't abide it when dads are heralded as being wonderful for doing something that should come naturally, like changing a nappy.*

Chris: *I don't feel that it is portrayed in any light to any great extent. Not with babies anyway. TV and glossies always portray women with babies and that is mainly centred around advertising. Most movies I've seen with the fatherhood theme* (About A Boy, Big Daddy, Three Men and a Baby) *all portray men as failures who can only cope when there is a female influence around.*

Mark: *Bumbling but well-meaning dad is corrected by wise and learned wife while he acts like a big child; i.e. fairly accurate.*

Chapter Twelve

Mates (Remember Them?)

WARNING:
Your Mates' Reactions Are Not Always Joyful...

There is one thing you probably already know that is going to happen after your baby is born: no mate of yours is going to turn up at your house with baby clothes, some baby-feeding gadget or a digital camera demanding a 'picture'. CORRECTION: there is a possibility that one or more of your mates will turn up at your house when the baby is born, and they may even bring gifts and so forth, but only because they've been dragged there with their broody girlfriend (or mum or sister) and they really, really do not want to be there.

They will stand at the door and look embarrassed, or phone you up to explain why they are coming over, speaking in serious tones. They would like to say, 'I don't want to be here,' or, 'My girlfriend is going baby-crazy and wants to see your baby,' but they can't because they don't want to be rude to you and your missus. Plus, it will put them in deep water with their missus if she finds out. What is worse is that when your mate and his girlfriend do turn up, he is really embarrassed. If his girlfriend goes into goo-goo heaven as she talks babies with your partner, he will nearly die of shame and not even the offer of a beer and the chance to talk complete bollocks with someone he has known for ages can hide the fact that he wants to RUN.

They know, as you once knew, that new babies are contagious! The arrival of babies in a busy room or work office can provoke near mass hysteria in females of a breeding age. Once women get it into their heads that they want one, once the ticks and tocks of that biological clock start getting louder, then your mate knows his carefree days are numbered.

When a bloke has a baby, his mates just naturally start to ignore him. It is not as if you become some sort of pariah or totally *persona non grata*, like if you got caught shagging a mate's girlfriend, or decided to 'come out of the closet' and move in with Nigel or, worse, bought an old Fiat Panda, but a bloke with a new baby can find himself left out in the cold. Your mates, who in your old bachelor days would risk life and limb to rescue you from the beer-goggled pursuit of unattractive females in countless clubs and bars across the country, or provide the list of suitable alibis you needed to watch more than one football match in a week, suddenly seem to desert you. Now they don't even call.

This is not as terrible as it seems and it is usually temporary. To be honest, you may have become rather boring during the run-up to the birth and used up a few favours. But the main reason is that all your mates are giving you some space because they know that you now have new priorities. They know you cannot go out as much as you once did. They know that you are tired as the baby keeps waking you up. They know that you have to help the missus. They know you are up to your ears in nappies, wipes and baby excrement. If you are like most couples with a new baby you probably don't have much cash either. The last thing they want to do is ring up and say, 'Are you coming out on Tuesday?' only to hear the sad and pathetic voice of one of their mates first have to ask (beg) to go and then be told, 'No.' So rule one of post-baby relations with your mates is if you want to go out, you call them. Or tell them when you are able to go out. But remember when you do get out not to go overboard – as this will just jeopardize any chance of another night off next month. And secondly, remember the 'Male-to-Male Baby Etiquette.'

Male-To-Male Baby Etiquette

Photos
You may carry a picture of your baby, but only one. It is better if it is a small and inconsequential photo, like a passport photo or one carried on your mobile. You may show it the first time you see your mates but ONLY on request thereafter. If shown a photo of your mate's baby, always say it looks lovely/cute even if it looks ugly. You may also allow your mates permission to use the photo of your baby to chat up women. (A baby picture can bring spectacular results for your mates with large groups of women as they can use the 'I want kids' card and get the great 'potential dad' vote by association.)

In General Conversation
The rule for blokes discussing their kids is to convey information in a very limited, very neutral way. Items need to be newsworthy, such as, 'My two-year-old just destroyed

my DVD player,' but never gushing or emotional unless you are with the wife/girlfriend and you are using it to build up brownie points. (Using babies as an excuse not to do something is also lame, unless it is true or unless you really, really cannot face going into the office and you need to take a sicky.) Moaning about nappies, sleepless nights and lack of sex is acceptable if discussed humorously. You may also take the piss out of any mate who has been forced to visit you to see the baby by his girlfriend, with a lot of, 'You're next, mate' banter.

Asking for Serious Advice
This is totally acceptable. The only way a bloke can learn something is to be told how to do it, be shown how to do it or watch how to do it, so if you need to ask one of your mates who has been down the road of fatherhood already, ask.

Hand-Me-Downs and Baby Stuff
Never but *never* ask other blokes for hand-me-downs or baby stuff. First, your missus is going to fill your loft and shed with as much stuff as she can lay her hands on. Second, if a bloke can, he will empty his loft and shed of baby stuff by giving it to you. Third, whatever you collect from another bloke is likely to be a) complete rubbish, b) the wrong thing, or c) for the wrong age/gender child.

Letting Go

Be it a social function, or a work conference, or an impromptu work night out that quickly became a night of debauchery, or a mate's stag do (that *will* be a night of debauchery)... chances are, whilst the little one is still, well, little, that you're going to have to go off and do something on your own that is invariably quite boozy, a little bit exciting and very expensive, whilst the love of your life is left very much on babysitting duty. It is going to involve a day, and let's be honest, probably a night away from your baby – how hard can it be?

You can beat yourself up about it and even decide not to go, or you can accept that you have a life outside babies and can and should still do most of the things you did before you had children. It will be hard, but at the end of the day you are, and should be, independent of your children... There really is nothing wrong with maintaining friendships that involve a number of people travelling vast tracts of the country to meet up every six months or so – it is only if it becomes weekly or monthly that you (or, more accurately, your partner) would have something to worry about. Equally, if you're allowed to go off and meet your chums every once in a while, then as a courtesy, the same option and freedom (and encouragement to take up on it) should be offered to your partner. Looking after a baby on your own is hard, but not impossible. Try it! You might like it.

The Big Blow-Out

The first night you get all to yourself (and a few others down the line in the foreseeable future), are likely to result in you going completely off the rails. I mean *really* going off the rails. It's not your fault, it really isn't. Yes, you're still a responsible parent, yes, you still love your new baby and yes, you would never ordinarily behave like this... except you've just become a dad, and that, without a shadow of a doubt, is the most profound thing in the world. So understand right away that you will end up going out on the piss; you will get hammered and you will feel better for it. But, most importantly, make sure your spectacular double-pike fall off the wagon is nowhere near the residence of your partner and your child.

As much as we like to believe that we handled the birth of our child with the candour and good grace of a saint, we didn't. OK, on the surface we might have been as cool as they come, have interacted well with the midwife and generally got on with all involved – and there was no doubting the absolute joy the first time we saw our first-born. But that said, it was also a shock to the system – the blood, the tears, the sweat, (the poo!), the painful close-ups of your partner's anatomy exposed to the world and stretched beyond all recognition... It has left us scarred and upset.

For some, the opportunity to blot it all out for a while presents itself within a week or so of the birth; for others, myself included, it could be over a year later. But I promise you, the blow-out will happen, and it may be during the most unexpected of events... I'm talking about the informal get-together of friends, or the 'let's meet up for a few beers' event that invariably leads to total and utter carnage...

The important thing to remember is that no matter how 'sensible' you usually are, no matter how 'out-of-character' this is, there will come the time when you throw caution to the wind and indulge in a night of selfish abandon. Yes, over the course of the evening you will end up as a shell of the man we knew before about six o'clock. You will be drinking to excess and loving every minute of it. It might all end in nausea, on your mate's floor, or under a bush in the park; but this is fatherhood. This is hedonism, revisited.

I'll Just Check My Diary

All those years that you lived by the maxim of 'mates before meat' mean nothing now. In fairness, you probably regret ever coining or using such phrases because in principle, your mates have now become secondary to your family. Never a bad thing, but always easier to accept if your friends have children as well. Your diary will always be full when you have a baby. Baby showers, first birthday parties, christenings galore. And then before you know it...

The Second Birthday Party!

How did this happen so fast? A moment ago you were sneaking a peek at the 'maternity swimwear' feature in your partner's pregnancy magazine. Then came the labour, still so brutally fresh in your memory, followed quickly by life with a newborn. You've bought a load of baby stuff, lost some more hair, possibly changed jobs or maybe even been promoted and now, in what seems a matter of moments later, it's the second anniversary of your baby's arrival in the world. How? What? When?

Second birthdays, for me anyway, are pretty monumental occasions. The first birthday is a bit crap, really – it's more of a chance to invite your mates round and have a few drinks. The focus of the attention is asleep and not really in a position to actually thank anyone for the deluge of gifts received. This time, it's different. She's walking, talking, shouting, screaming and knows exactly what presents are, and whom they're for, but is still none-the-wiser about the fine art of saying 'Thank you.'

The second birthday party is the first occasion where the supposed 'differences' in ability between child peers begins to become a bit hazy – at this stage of their development, a few months one way or another is less profound than the difference between, say, a six-month-old and a ten-month-old. Personalities are beginning to show, accents beginning to be apparent and their attitude is gearing itself up for the whole wacky world of the Terrible Twos.

Two-year-old girls will more often than not be aware that they're the centre of attention from early morning and be more than happy to dress up in their nice party frock and act as bouncer on the door, ensuring that all who enter the venue come bearing gifts. Two-year-old boys will be less keen to dress up, unless dressing up means a pirate/Spider-man/Bob/Thomas (delete as applicable) t-shirt is the order of the day. They're little people now, no longer babies. Let's dim the lights, turn down the music and soak up the scene for a second:

And there she is, dressed up in her party frock, demanding presents from everyone as they come into the house. Your beautiful child, so much larger than the baby that was pressed into your arms, swaddled in a white towel, two years ago today. It's all gone so fast, and surprisingly, so well. You've coped, you've succeeded, with only one or two major scares; and now she's pouring a glass of lemonade all over someone's mum. Nice.

Childrearing really is the most rewarding experience we can have on this planet. Non-believers can keep their single life, ability to go to the pub with friends at the drop of the hat and lie-ins on a Sunday. Those days are now long-gone for us dads. You will probably be cleaning up some child's sick off the floor before the day is through – too much jelly and ice cream and not enough savouries. But, to be honest, it doesn't matter. It all comes so naturally now. In a weird way, it's kind of fun. The adventure really does continue – she won't be a baby or a toddler for much longer; in just over a year you will be walking her to pre-school. Now there's a sobering thought...

One of the questions that I asked my interviewees was: 'Is there any advice you would give to new dads?' I leave you with Mark's answer:

If you're surviving, you're doing it right. There really is no right or wrong as far as I'm concerned to being a dad, as long as you're not making life miserable for your kids. So I'd pass on just those two bits of advice. Actually those two and 'Don't sweat the small stuff.' Have you ever noticed in some families of four or more how it's the eldest who turns out to be a drug dealer while their siblings are all relatively sane? It's because the parents were too strict with the first one. You have to guide them about what's right and wrong but you can't squash them as they're little people in their own right. So that's three. Now I think about it, most dads I know slowly weaned themselves off being so self-absorbed the longer they went on. Less time on the PS2, more time on the Lego. Ok, that's four, but now I realize that you don't actually have to follow any rules with kids. So scrap all that. Love them, be obsessed with their happiness and everything else falls into place.

Afterword

No guide is ever definitive, but I hope that *The Bloke's Guide to Babies* has helped you understand some of the changes in you, your partner, your child and your lives. Children are remarkable and you'll never get tired of looking at them, caring for them and worrying about them. There will never be a book written that will categorically list your own personal experience week by week but I hope that you can relate to most of the aspects I've covered here. Luckily, each child is unique and that is what is so great about being a father.

To all dads out there taking an active role in their child's development: congratulations and keep up the good work.

Jon Smith
Valencia, Spain

Websites Of Interest:
www.jonsmith.net
www.justdads.co.uk
www.blokesguide.com
www.hayhouse.co.uk

Useful Contacts

There are both good and bad sources of information available on the Internet, in the telephone directory, and advertised on bad photocopies for 20p a week in the local newsagents. The Internet, especially, is a constantly changing phenomenon and therefore good (and bad) sites are forever popping up and dropping off. Here follows a list of, in my opinion, useful websites, telephone numbers and addresses that relate to specific chapters in this book. All links were checked at the time of going to press.

Pregnancy and Beyond
www.mothersbliss.co.uk
www.babycentre.com
www.parentlineplus.org.uk; 0800 800 2222

Relationships
www.relate.org.uk

Post-Natal Depression
MAMA (Meet a Mum Association) 0208 768 0123
Association of Postnatal Illness 0207 386 0868

BUPA Childcare
www.bupa.co.uk/childcare

NHS direct
www.nhsdirect.nhs.uk

Nappy Suppliers (and Cleaning)

www.spiritofnature.co.uk
www.babykind.co.uk
www.pure_nappies.com

General

www.blokesguide.com
www.justdads.co.uk

Suggested Further Reading

Gina Ford *The Complete Sleep Guide for Contented Babies and Toddlers* (Vermilion, 2006)

Stephen Giles *You're the Daddy*
(White Ladder Press, 2006)

Richard Ferber *Solve Your Child's Sleep Problems*
(Dorling Kindersley Publishers Ltd, 1986)

Gina Ford *The New Contented Little Baby Book*
(Vermilion, 2006)

Deborah Jackson *Three in a Bed: The Benefits of Sleeping With Your Baby* (Bloomsbury Publishing, 1999)

Christopher Green *New Toddler Taming*
(Vermilion, 2006)

Acknowledgements

Without the birth of my children, Alia and Ronin, I would not be the person I am today, nor would I have had reason to write this book. Alia and Ronin are a huge inspiration to both my wife and me. I hope they both grow to realize that their existence, from conception to now, has made a massive and positive difference to our lives.

A huge thank you to Lisa, my wife, for putting up with my ambitions and supporting me along each stage of the way – and for allowing me to share many real-life anecdotes throughout the book.

This book would not have been possible without the detailed, sometimes harrowing, often funny, and incredibly insightful testimonies of the 85 fathers interviewed. Thank you all.

And finally, a thank you to you, the reader. By buying this book you prove that there is an appetite for more male-directed information about parenting. Which also proves that some of us 'blokes' do want to be involved and included in every stage of our child's life.

Also by Jon Smith

The Bloke's Guide to Pregnancy (Hay House, 2004)

The Bloke's Guide to Baby Gadgets (Hay House, 2006)

The Bloke's Guide to Getting Hitched (Hay House, 2007)

Toytopia (Wrecking Ball Press, 2004)

Smarter Business Start-Ups (Infinite Ideas Limited, 2004)

Web Sites That Work (Infinite Ideas Limited, 2004)

Get into Bed with Google: Top Ranking Search Optimisation Techniques (Infinite Ideas Limited, 2008)

Words of praise for
The Bloke's Guide
to Pregnancy

'Excellent advice and information on everything
– from options on the type of birth and medical
interventions, to being the partner's voice
during the birth.' *Relate Magazine*

'Jon Smith gives his lowdown on what men
should expect over the happy but stressful
nine-month countdown.' *Daily Express*

'Right-on.' *YOU* magazine, *Mail on Sunday*

Words of praise for
The Bloke's 100 Top Tips
for Surviving Pregnancy

100 bite-sized chunks that even the most
book-phobic bloke will be able to digest.

'Easy to digest ... the book covers everything a
first-time father-to-be will want to know about
pregnancy but may be too embarrassed to ask'
Junior Pregnancy & Baby

Hay House Titles of Related Interest

How to Stop Your Kids Watching Too Much TV, Spending Hours on the Computer, Wasting Days on the Game Boy and Endlessly Texting Friends, etc...,
by Teresa Orange & Louise O'Flynn

Baby Sign Language Basics: Early Communication for Hearing Babies and Toddlers, by Monta Z. Briant

Kate and Emily's Guide to Single Parenting,
by Kate Ford and Emily Abbott

Sign, Sing and Play!: Fun Signing Activities,
by Monta Briant

How To Be A Great Single Dad, by Theo Theobald

Notes

Notes

Notes

Notes

JOIN THE HAY HOUSE FAMILY

As the leading self-help, mind, body and spirit publisher in the UK, we'd like to welcome you to our family so that you can enjoy all the benefits our website has to offer.

 EXTRACTS from a selection of your favourite author titles

 COMPETITIONS, PRIZES & SPECIAL OFFERS Win extracts, money off, downloads and so much more

 LISTEN to a range of radio interviews and our latest audio publications

 CELEBRATE YOUR BIRTHDAY An inspiring gift will be sent your way

 LATEST NEWS Keep up with the latest news from and about our authors

 ATTEND OUR AUTHOR EVENTS Be the first to hear about our author events

 iPHONE APPS Download your favourite app for your iPhone

 HAY HOUSE INFORMATION Ask us anything, all enquiries answered

join us online at **www.hayhouse.co.uk**

 292B Kensal Road, London W10 5BE
T: 020 8962 1230 E: info@hayhouse.co.uk

We hope you enjoyed this Hay House book.
If you would like to receive a free catalogue featuring additional
Hay House books and products, or if you would like information
about the Hay Foundation, please contact:

Hay House UK Ltd
292B Kensal Rd • London W10 5BE
Tel: (44) 20 8962 1230; Fax: (44) 20 8962 1239
www.hayhouse.co.uk

***

Published and distributed in the United States of America by:
Hay House, Inc. • PO Box 5100 • Carlsbad, CA 92018-5100
Tel.: (1) 760 431 7695 or (1) 800 654 5126;
Fax: (1) 760 431 6948 or (1) 800 650 5115
www.hayhouse.com

Published and distributed in Australia by:
Hay House Australia Ltd • 18/36 Ralph St • Alexandria NSW 2015
Tel.: (61) 2 9669 4299; Fax: (61) 2 9669 4144
www.hayhouse.com.au

Published and distributed in the Republic of South Africa by:
Hay House SA (Pty) Ltd • PO Box 990 • Witkoppen 2068
Tel./Fax: (27) 11 467 8904 • www.hayhouse.co.za

Published and distributed in India by:
Hay House Publishers India • Muskaan Complex • Plot No.3
B-2 • Vasant Kunj • New Delhi – 110 070.
Tel.: (91) 11 41761620; Fax: (91) 11 41761630.
www.hayhouse.co.in

Distributed in Canada by:
Raincoast • 9050 Shaughnessy St • Vancouver, BC V6P 6E5
Tel.: (1) 604 323 7100; Fax: (1) 604 323 2600

***

Sign up via the Hay House UK website to receive the Hay House
online newsletter and stay informed about what's going on with
your favourite authors. You'll receive bimonthly announcements
about discounts and offers, special events, product highlights,
free excerpts, giveaways, and more!
www.hayhouse.co.uk